Issues in the Social Sciences Series: 5

Series Editors: Anne Boran and David Charles Ford

Fragmenting
Family?

In the Same Series

Fragmenting Family?

*Papers from a Conference held at
the University of Chester,
November 2004*

Edited by David Charles Ford

Chester Academic Press

First published 2010
by Chester Academic Press
University of Chester
Parkgate Road
Chester CH1 4BJ

Printed and bound in the UK by the
LIS Print Unit
University of Chester
Cover designed by the
LIS Graphics Team
University of Chester

A catalogue record for this book is available from the
British Library

ISBN 978-1-905929-78-8

CONTENTS

CONTRIBUTORS

Professor Anne Barlow is Professor of Family Law and Policy at the University of Exeter. The main focus of her research has been on how law should respond to the needs of changing families and changing social norms. She has directed and co-directed a number of empirical socio-legal projects funded by the Nuffield Foundation, the Ministry of Justice and the ESRC. Her recent publications include: 'Cohabiting relationships and money and property: the legal backdrop' (2008), *Journal of Socio-Economics, 37* (2), 502-18; 'Cohabitation and the law: myths, money and the media', in A. Park et al. (Eds.), *British social attitudes: The 24th report,* London: Sage (2008; with C. Burgoyne, E. Clery & J. Smithson); and *Cohabitation, marriage and the law* (2005; with S. Duncan, G. James, & A. Park).

Professor Simon Duncan is Professor of Comparative Social Policy at the University of Bradford. He has researched on the "new family"; motherhood and work-life balance; the geography of family formations; and comparative gender inequality. He is currently researching "Living Apart Together" and personal life in Britain and Sweden in the 1950s. Recent publications include *Analysing families* (2004 ed.; with A. Carling & R. Edwards); *Cohabitation, marriage and the law* (2005; with A. Barlow, G. James & A. Park) and 'New families? Tradition and change in partnering and relationships' in A. Park et al. (Eds.), *British social attitudes: The 24th report,* London: Sage (2008; with M. Phillips).

Vicki Ford is a couples' counsellor and psychosexual therapist of many years standing. She is the author of *Overcoming Sexual Problems,* published by Constable and Robinson (2005) as part of their successful 'Overcoming'

Contributors

series. Vicki is currently working for the NHS as a Cognitive Behavioural Therapist on the Improving Access to Psychological Therapies [IAPT] scheme.

Professor Gill Hague is Professor of Violence Against Women Studies and Co-Director of the Violence Against Women Research Group at the University of Bristol. She has worked on domestic violence for over 35 years and has had a pioneering role in developing gender violence research in the UK. Gill has conducted a large number of research projects on the issue in many countries including India, South Africa, Canada, Kurdistan and Uganda. She recently led both a large collaborative study on how to involve domestic violence survivors in service development, and the first ever national UK study of disabled women and domestic violence. She is currently working with activist NGOs in Africa and the Middle East on marriage rites, poverty, and domestic abuse, and on "honour"-based violence. She has produced over 90 publications on violence against women.

Dr Grace James is Reader in Law at the University of Reading. Her main research focus is family-friendly employment law policies and anti-discrimination law. Recent publications include *The legal regulation of pregnancy and parenting in the labour market* (Routledge-Cavendish, 2009) and her co-authored book (with A. Barlow, S. Duncan & A. Park), *Cohabitation, marriage and the law* (Hart Publishing, 2005).

Julie Lewis obtained a First Class Degree in Women's Studies at Liverpool John Moores University in 2003, after seven years of part-time study whilst working full-time. She is currently Co-Chair of the Sefton branch of the Fawcett Society, is on the board of Sefton Women's and

Children's Aid, and also works for Sefton Council for Voluntary Service.

Susanna Lloyd completed an M.Phil. at Liverpool John Moores University in 2008, focusing on women's reproductive health in Nepal. She currently teaches research methods at the University of Plymouth.

Dr Nancy Loucks is Chief Executive of the Edinburgh-based charity Families Outside. Her publications include *"Anything goes"* (1995), *Young people in custody in Scotland* (2000), *Just visiting?* (2002) and *Recidivism amongst serious violent and sexual offenders* (2002).

Dr Katy Radford has a Ph.D. in Social Anthropology. Formerly employed by Save the Children in Northern Ireland as acting head of policy and research, she is currently a Research Fellow in the School of Sociology, Social Policy and Social Work at Queen's University Belfast, where she works on issues of social inclusion for older people in rural areas. She is an associate of the Institute for Conflict Research, a not-for-profit organisation committed to community development principles and for whom she conducts policy-related research and consultations with vulnerable adults and youths. Katy has a particular interest in working with victims and survivors of conflict and with those from minority ethnic and faith-based communities.

Dr Catrin Smith is currently a Lecturer in Criminology at the School of Criminology and Criminal Justice, Griffith University, Queensland, Australia, having previously been Reader in Criminology at the University of Chester. She has been grant holder and principal investigator on a number of research projects, with funding from the Scottish Office, the High Security Psychiatric Services Commissioning

Board and the British Academy. She has completed studies on teenage sexuality in Scotland, health issues for incarcerated women (UK and USA), aspects of care and control at Ashworth High Security (Special) Psychiatric Hospital, and cultural aspects of female injecting drug use (North Wales and Texas).

Dr Kay Standing is a Senior Lecturer in Sociology at Liverpool John Moores University. She was project manager for the ESF projects, 'Combining work and family life in the UK and Netherlands' and the Equilibrium work-life balance training project. She is currently involved in a DELPHE-funded project on gender and education in Nepal and Bangladesh.

Dr Louise Wattis is a Lecturer in Criminology at the University of Teesside. Her research interests cover both sociology and criminology and are united by a focus on gender. Her current interests are fear of crime and identity and the impact of economic transformations on working experiences and policy.

Dr David Charles Ford (editor) is a Senior Lecturer and Programme Leader for Sociology in the Department of Social and Communication Studies at the University of Chester. His primary research area of interest is in social theory, with a particular focus upon contemporary social inequality and disadvantage. His current research is concerned with explaining the socio-economic polarisation of smoking and he has published a number of articles on this subject. David's teaching commitments include being module leader for the Department's 'Sociological Imagination', 'Shaping of Society', 'Sociology of Health, Disease and Medicine' and 'Advanced Social Theory' modules.

ACKNOWLEDGEMENTS

Many thanks go to all of those who have contributed towards the making of this book. Sincerest thanks to the volume's authors for their impressively informative and insightful contributions to the academic debate. A special thank you to the staff of the Department of Social and Communication Studies for the help and support given in organising and making the conference a success, and also to our students for choosing such an engaging conference focus, and for their active involvement in research and debate and their clear enthusiasm for the subject. Finally, very sincere thanks and appreciation go to Peter Williams and Sarah Griffiths, Editorial Advisors of Chester Academic Press, for their invaluable help and support in preparing this volume for publication.

INTRODUCTION

Fifty years ago, C. Wright Mills famously called for a "sociological imagination" as "our most needed quality of mind" (1959, p. 13). The sheer pace of social change generated by the global capitalist political economy subjected people to immense anxiety as "cherished values" and deeply embedded beliefs about the way to live life that had been previously relied upon were increasingly threatened, undermined and discarded. He distinguishes between "private troubles" and "public issues", between our autonomy as human agents and structural relations beyond our direct control. A sociological imagination has the potential to distinguish between structural social upheaval and individual biography as the dynamic context within which people struggle to make sense of their lives.

Social change has indeed been astonishing and continues unabated at a relentless pace, and there are many examples where very deeply established and powerful beliefs have been overturned or abandoned. For just one example, during the 1960s I recall a day at school when the playground reverberated with the rumour that the parents of one boy may have been unmarried at his time of birth. Tangible shock and horror accompanied a shared acute awareness of the burden of the social stigma attached to the label of "bastard" (perhaps akin to Marley's chains, although not at all of his own forging in this instance) that the unfortunate individual would henceforth carry forward with him through life. I was very grateful indeed that my own parents had adhered to the "correct" order of proceedings. It is very revealing of a rapidly changing social structure that my own children have all chosen to marry after the birth of children, and yet my grandchildren will carry forward none of the stigma previously indelibly

1

attached to this omission. A debilitating social stigma understood by everyone has now been cast aside and consigned to history.

All of us would agree that in the above instance change has been progressive and a thoroughly good thing. Nonetheless, anxieties surrounding a perceived loosening in social ties and moral values, and what this will all mean in relation to our futures, abound. It is also evident that the future of the family is firmly placed at the very heart of public concerns in this regard. Discourses bemoaning the loss of "old-fashioned" values are commonplace. Lowering levels of personal commitment are often said to be at the root of unprecedented rates of divorce and family dissolution. A regrettable decline in the standard of discipline is said to significantly account for a perceived rise in youth delinquency and anti-social behaviour, and even violent crime. These, and so many more supposed attacks on the family of a supposedly "golden past" merge with the contemporary explosion of diversity in family arrangements and relationships into a palpable and widely shared disquiet that the decline and decay of "family values" signals the disintegration and perhaps even the impending dissolution of the family. It is this widespread perception of "fragmenting family" that is the focus of the critique in this volume.

Fragmenting Family? is the fifth volume in the *Issues in the Social Sciences Series*. The book is a compilation of selected papers, aimed primarily at an undergraduate student audience, delivered at the Department of Social and Communication Studies' Annual Conference at the University of Chester in November 2004. This annual event emerges from the Conference module, which is a Level 5 compulsory requirement to the Sociology programme. Each year students select the topic for the conference and expert participants in the field are invited to present academic papers, in this case to explore the complex ways in which family relationships have changed or are changing in order to test the widely-held belief that the family is in the process of fragmenting. The result was a fascinating and informative diverse range of analyses that stimulated a lively intellectual debate, which is reproduced in this book. Each chapter advances our knowledge about the ways in which the family can be understood to be evolving at the interface between the individual family group and the broader historical social structural change. This is the juncture at which the dilemmas of everyday family life are acted out, and which may then add, albeit in some small way, towards future social change.

Although interdisciplinary in nature, all of the analyses penetrate the level of complexity underlying family change to add to our understanding, and thus they contribute incrementally to Wright Mills "sociological imagination". The book incorporates a broad cross section of key areas of contention that are explored from a range of vantage points across the structure/agency continuum. There are some significant associations between the topics which have helped to dictate the chapter order. Chapters 2, 3, and 4 adopt a gender perspective and provide a specific focus on women in families. Chapters 2, 4, 5, and 6 each invite us into private "hidden worlds" that are exposed to the added impediment of social stigma and shame. Chapters 1 and 7 focus primarily on adult or couple relationships located more towards the mainstream of family life and social experience. These two chapters take a particularly robust and optimistic stance in relation to the central conference theme, that contemporary family change does not constitute a process of fragmentation.

The keynote speaker, Simon Duncan, embarks directly to the heart of the debate. "Why Don't They Marry? Commitment and Cohabitation in 21st Century Britain", explores the rise in popularity of unmarried heterosexual cohabitation. The sexual revolutions of the sixties helped set the scene for a more permissive society, but the freedom for couples to choose cohabitation over marriage would remain highly circumscribed by class and other factors until relatively recently. Young men and women of the previous generation, particularly those of working-class origin, would have experienced considerable social pressure exerted by parents and significant others to marry, as the "right" thing to do. This pressure has largely dissipated and no longer exists for the vast majority of the population across the social spectrum. Cohabitation is now widely regarded as an acceptable practice, at least as an option or prelude to marriage. However, in its wake remains the reservation that the rise of cohabitation is reflecting social decline and an abandonment of core "family values", especially commitment.

In a well-crafted critical examination of the everyday lived experience of the contemporary cohabiting couple, Duncan successfully overturns the premise that cohabitation is indicative of reduced commitment. Through challenging a range of widely-held assumptions, Duncan reveals that private commitment is indeed central to an adequate understanding of cohabitation, especially among the under-35 age group. It is those that have equated commitment with marriage that display the "ignorance". When comparing like with like, and adjusting for age, most cohabitants are likely to show as much commitment as married people. Duncan concludes that public anxiety and government thinking is out-of-step with the reality by mistakenly identifying cohabitation as an inferior family form, rather than recognising the similarities between marriage and cohabitation, and the ethical honesty underlying cohabitation as an alternative way of demonstrating care and commitment between adults and to their children. In sum, it is entirely erroneous to ascribe the rise in cohabitation as a marker of family decay or of a declining commitment between couples. Duncan's chapter informs us that changes in family arrangements do not necessarily lead to social decline, and can be fully explained and accounted for in terms of the wider changes in social relations and the social structure.

It is important to note that the desire for family structures to remain constant carries with it an inbuilt assumption that "old values" were qualitatively better. This may be a rather doubtful and perhaps even a dangerous premise. Whilst Mrs Thatcher famously drew upon an image of the "Victorian family values" of a "golden age" that has since lost its way, the Victorian reality for the majority of the population, families and children, was very harsh indeed. Further, an over-rigid family structure can provide a cloak for other horrors. The strong emphasis upon discipline in the past chimed in harmony with a rigid and stifling patriarchal structure that acted to deny women and children a voice, and also helped to disguise and perhaps even legitimate bullying and abuse. Do we really want to go back to a "children (and women) are to be seen, and not heard" mentality?

The next three chapters adopt a gendered perspective to focus on women. The first of these is on the subject of domestic violence. In "Fragmenting Families: The Devastating Legacy of Domestic Violence", Gill Hague applies a social policy perspective in order to highlight the progress achieved in this field of endeavour through political activity, instigated by the "second wave" feminists and continued by women activists up to the present day. In a comprehensive and broad sweeping analysis, Hague sets the scene by juxtaposing the ideology of the family as "a haven in a heartless world", to the disturbing reality of the timeless prevalence and horrific nature of domestic violence within it. The family is not, and never has been, a "safe haven" for far too many women and children across the social spectrum and in all types and varieties of family. Nonetheless, she presents a tentatively optimistic view. Throughout history, domestic violence has been heavily shrouded in secrecy and silence. However, over recent decades the efforts of women activists worldwide have succeeded in uncovering the ugly reality of domestic violence and abuse, and thus have transformed understanding and raised levels of awareness.

Hague makes evident the difficulty of providing a clear and precise definition of such a wide-ranging phenomenon. Domestic violence takes a myriad of forms and includes physical, sexual, emotional/psychological and economic abuses, and combinations of these, enacted in the most intimate of relationships. Domestic violence incorporates multiple types of assault, attack and injury, is frighteningly common and on a global scale that crosses all cultures and classes. A brief review of a wide range of theories that attempt to explain domestic violence establishes that most are inadequate and provide only a partial or a very limited purchase on the causes of domestic violence. The author advocates a gender-aware feminist approach that identifies power and patterns of domination and control within gender relations as key. Crucially, these are the theories that feed into social policy initiatives and practices.

The author cautions against interpreting the transformation of service provision over the last 30 years as evidence that the devastation caused to women (and some men) by domestic violence is likely to come to an end any time soon. Rather, she advocates that we gain inspiration from the achievements of women activists that have provided a vision to be aspired to of a future in which women and children will be safe and free from the devastating impact of domestic violence and abuse.

The second of the chapters to provide a gendered analysis examines work-life balance. Louise Wattis, Kay Standing, Susanna Lloyd and Julie Lewis, in "The Gendered Nature of Work-Life Balance", present a telling critique that frames the lived-life experience of women as they struggle to manage work, care and family life in the face of government legislative change, supposedly enacted to support women and families.

The authors argue that UK policy directives on working arrangements are aligned much more closely to a US labour market that emphasises deregulation and a free market over the interests of employees. It is this tension between employee and employer interests which generates contradiction and inconsistency that helps to undermine the effectiveness and utility of government legislation. Policy is further compromised by the importation of underlying cultural assumptions regarding women's social roles, especially the expectation that women take primary responsibility in the nurturing and domestic spheres. The upshot of this is that the raft of New Labour so called "family-friendly" legislation contributes towards the perpetuation of the gendering of work and care practices.

A comparative analysis is skilfully deployed to show that the UK government "family-friendly" policy not only fails to meet its prescribed ends, but in important ways is relatively "unenlightened" in relation to that of some other European countries that pay considerably greater attention to the place of care. However, the deeper social structure, even in these countries, helps to ensure the continuation of labour market inequalities and the gendered nature of caring.

This is not to claim that progress has not been made. Family-friendly policies have produced undeniable benefits. However, a prioritising of economic productivity and the persistence of traditional work cultures have also helped to maintain gendered working practices. In effect, while lip service is paid to gender equity, working practices continue to incorporate robust patriarchal elements that protect and maintain the status quo to ensure gendered outcomes in work and care. All of this leaves women struggling in a system heavily weighted against them. Decisions and dilemmas of family life must be reconciled within a rigid and uncompromising framework that allows precious little latitude for significant social movement in the gendered nature of the work-life-care balance.

The following three chapters are linked by the incorporation of a particularly unpalatable constituent into the family mix. In common with the earlier chapter on domestic violence, these chapters depict families that struggle against social stigma and shame. These are private "hidden worlds" that are pushed far outside the nostalgic Victorian view of family harmony. These are worlds that are encased in silence and often overlooked, shunned by most people and seen as dangerous or distasteful. Nonetheless, these are also worlds in which people struggle to bring up their children against a backdrop of social isolation.

The first of these chapters, and the final chapter to adopt a specifically female focus, is "Maternal Drug Use in the Context of Family Life: Accounts of Mexican-American Female Injecting Drug Users and Their Children", by Catrin Smith. In a detailed and often moving analysis, Smith invites us into the unpredictable and hazardous family environment of the female heroin addict. Here we see secretive and socially isolated family groups that occupy a chaotic and risky environment. These families are also thoroughly enmeshed in an unenviable array of poverty-associated markers. Nonetheless, the in-depth interviews reveal the fundamental centrality of family and the importance attached to family ties as the heroin-addicted women struggle to negotiate the maternal role in the face of poverty, violence, criminality and, perhaps above all, family instability.

Smith reveals how culture and gender expectations impact particularly cruelly upon these women and their families. Severe social stigma is attached to the female heroin addict in the Mexican-American culture, especially those who are mothers. One outcome of the consequent need to remain secretive is to propel the mothers, and their children, even deeper into a life of social exclusion and social isolation. Another is to actively impede them from participating in the intervention programmes designed to help them. Certainly, cultural condemnation is a major causal agent in preventing these women from seeking help.

Smith calls for a greater awareness, which could allow recognition of the fact that maternal drug use is perhaps predominantly an "effect" of disadvantage rather than its "cause". A clearer recognition of this fact should allow a shift in thinking to enable the development of a culturally sensitive intervention strategy designed to better facilitate these women's recovery.

The next chapter is entitled "And Stay Out! Hoods and Paramilitarised Youth: Exiling and Punishment Beatings", by Katy Radford. In a thoroughly thought-provoking chapter, Radford captures yet another largely hidden world. A world in which brutal punishments, including beatings, shootings and exiling, have been "naturalised" and are deeply embedded aspects of the social fabric and community reality. The author's primary focus is on youth offenders and young people in families that had received paramilitary warnings, beatings or exclusions.

Following a review of the theoretical literature, Radford proceeds to examine the dynamics of the relationships within a culture that has become tolerant of violence. To this, she applies a child-rights framework. A series of personal testimonies bring into full view the unpalatable reality of summary justice, abuses and rights violations. It is a salient point that the permanent physical and psychological scarring of people in the name of informal justice is meted out to victims by others within their own community.

The formation of the Hood and the Paramilitary identities is illuminating in this regard. The author informs us how limited choice on poor working-class estates channels many young people towards joining a Paramilitary organisation. Those that do not are susceptible to becoming marginalised and stigmatised as Hoods. It is this group that receives the beatings and the exilings for "offending behaviour" and persistent violations of community norms and values.

Radford introduces a very effective comparison between the paramilitary practice of exiling and the government's Anti-Social Behaviour Orders. Somewhat ironically perhaps, both contribute towards socially isolating vulnerable young people, without the provision of effective support. From a child-rights perspective, both forms of justice may be recognised as brutal. It becomes very clear that no government, paramilitary authority or community group is able, or willing to protect the human rights of the children and young people at risk. The author concludes that the tragedy of this highly politicised community is that all groups – families, workforces and elected authorities – are each potentially culpable for the perpetuation of the violation of children's rights through their very silence and inactivity.

The last of the series of chapters to uncover a neglected family group is by Nancy Loucks in "Prison Without Bars: The Impact of Imprisonment on Families". Imprisonment is most certainly a family experience. The author provides a detailed and very informative account of the difficulties experienced by the family from the perspective of the families on the outside. Loucks begins by bringing to the fore the dire consequences of imprisonment on the family unit. These cover an extraordinary range, but may well include severe and perhaps catastrophic economic and social problems, including loss of home. On top of all of this, families also have to manage the social stigma and shame that is attached to imprisonment, and an intense distress that often impacts upon the children of the family. The author brings home to us very clearly that the families serve out their own "stretch" on the outside when a family member is imprisoned.

A chronology of experiences, from initial arrest through to after release, identifies a range of factors which place tremendous strain upon the families. Clearly, these will differ in intensity and type from case to case, but what is particularly poignant is the overwhelming sense of powerlessness and bewilderment, abandonment and social isolation that is so suddenly thrust upon the families. It is, perhaps, not at all surprising that approaching half of those imprisoned lose contact with their families.

The author proceeds to point out the clear benefits attached to the maintenance of family ties. This can benefit all parties involved, and society more broadly. Benefits include improvements in prisoner behaviour, reductions in levels of recidivism, and an increased likelihood that families will reunite after release. Very encouragingly, there are a variety of initiatives in place, both from within the prison system and from external organisations. Families Outside, Action for Prisoners Families, Visitors' Centres and Family Support Officers each provide effective and much-needed support for families. However, resource provision tends to be patchy, and the communication of resources available to families is generally poor.

Loucks concludes that the priority is to strengthen existing resources. Consultation to allow a voice for the families and children is crucial in order to identify fresh avenues of service development to more effectively address the fear of stigma and lack of knowledge that families experience. In too many instances the bewildering array of pressures overwhelm the family unit to such a degree that they are incapable of engaging with what is available. The author calls for a reinvigorated effort to ensure that support for prisoners' families is firmly located at the very centre of prison policy.

The final chapter in this volume is by Vicki Ford: "When Two Becomes Three (Or More): The Effects of Parenthood on Relationships". Here we shift focus again towards couples that occupy a more visible space in the social mainstream. In a fascinating study, Ford presents a range of detailed relationship scenarios that bring into sharp focus the potential upheaval that can accompany the addition to the family unit of a child or children. Having a child is perhaps regarded as a misleadingly natural event, but it fanfares immediate, fundamental and irrevocable change that many couples are insufficiently prepared for. Becoming parents can undoubtedly bring couples together, but not in every case. The re-establishing of the couple equilibrium can be a delicate process as new demands for affection and attention can also lead to feelings of rejection.

Drawing on her extensive experience as a psychosexual therapist and relationship counsellor, Ford provides five intimate and intriguing case studies. These case studies illustrate the social and psychological complexity that can underlie relationship problems. A broad range of contemporary social issues are covered, including work-care balance, IVF treatment, depression and sexual difficulties, second marriages and stepfamilies, trust and bereavement, same-sex relationships, and social role reversals. In all cases, the dilemmas presented are complex, their impacts are often unforeseen, and they provide testimony to the potential for relationship disruption to strike with such depth and ferocity that professional help is sometimes required. Fortunately, counselling services are a resource that has gradually become more widely available and counselling nowadays carries little or no stigma attached to it.

Ford concludes on a positive note. She calls for better communication between couples as the best resource available in an age of huge social change and family diversity. As the case studies very effectively show, whilst coping with change can present huge challenges to couples and families, these challenges can be met, sometimes with a little help and support, and the eventual outcomes can be very positive.

What emerges as a whole from this volume is a very clear picture of the vital significance and overriding importance of family to people, even those whose family lives are lived in the most adverse of social situations. Catrin Smith captures this perfectly in her depiction of the women heroin addicts struggling to maintain the maternal role within an extremely intimidating and disadvantaged social environment, and again when the children take on the adult role to "look after" the family during periods of their mother's escalating drug use. The same is presented poignantly by Katy Radford as she describes how the young victims of informal justice would very often rather suffer severe beatings, in preference to exiling and the consequent separation from their families and communities.

Naturally, alongside dire social conditions go high rates of family attrition. Quite understandably, many families succumb to the intense pressures of an impoverished social environment. Nonetheless, many families do survive, some through drawing upon the resources made available. Nancy Loucks makes a convincing case for better support mechanisms for families in prison. These can provide substantial benefits in terms of the survival of families, but they also benefit society more broadly. Less recidivism and less disruption to children and families, and all that entails, is good news for all of us.

For those families who occupy a more comfortable social space free from the debilitations of poverty and social stigma, outcomes are, perhaps unsurprisingly, much more positive. Vicki Ford's analysis illustrates that, despite deep-rooted and difficult dilemmas that might be expected to test the love and commitment of any relationship, with appropriate support couples can overcome the challenges that confront them and transform their difficulties into positive outcomes. We can also draw on the positives from Simon Duncan's analysis. Here we see very committed young couples forging their future together amidst the contemporary diversity of family arrangements. The apparently counter-intuitive decision by couples to opt for cohabitation, despite a legal-political structure that denies them the same protection as married couples, is explained. Indeed, the eschewal of state, church, and traditional ceremony can be interpreted as indicative of a high level of commitment. To those couples who have opted for cohabitation, marriage may well be perceived as an inferior and instrumental practice that has more to do with social conformity and/or economic contract. At the heart of the decision to cohabit is a private emotional commitment between couples.

Some of the contributors to this volume have questioned the effectiveness of support mechanisms or social policies developed to help struggling families. In this context Nancy Loucks presents an interesting example of how the provider's social location can sometimes divert or dilute the impact of the provision. A qualitative distinction was identified between Visitors' Centres run by private or voluntary organisations which tended towards the provision of friendly support and help, and those run by the prison authorities that adopted a more instrumental approach concerned with practice and the efficient processing of the visitors.

Other authors have focused on questioning the effectiveness of government legislative interventions in their area of study. Louise Wattis and her colleagues highlight the short comings evident in New Labour "family-friendly" policy. Whilst the rhetoric is highly supportive of equitable social structural change to support working families, the policies clearly prioritise greater productivity over gender equality. The range of initiatives put forward by government provides little evidence of an awareness of the social and organisational structures that facilitate gendered divisions in work and care. As a consequence, women will continue in their dual roles, taking primary responsibility for care which is culturally undervalued, whilst participating in a structurally inequitable and highly gendered labour market.

The substantive point is that New Labour "family-friendly" policy, through a reinforcing of out-dated patriarchal structures inherent to work and care practices, hinders rather than enables social structural change in the direction of shared family arrangements in the bringing up of children. The government misses the opportunity to release the potential for flexibility and social structural realignment that already exists, because it does not recognise changes in family relationships that have actually happened and how people actually live their day to day lives across the spheres of work and family.

Fragmenting Family?

Gill Hague in her analysis makes evident the perennial shortages in provision of government agency resources for the victims of domestic violence. Katy Radford also points to the failure of government to support the human rights of the most vulnerable young people in the Northern Ireland context. In both of these instances, more robust action and increased resources are required from the state to fulfil its legal obligations to the most vulnerable in society through the development and implementation of sound public policies.

A final theme linking the chapters is poverty. Poverty is socially corrosive. The families depicted by Catrin Smith carry an extraordinary burden of social disadvantage, and yet the initiation into problematic substance abuse is very often a response to a traumatic life event. The persistent negative imagery surrounding maternal drug use here also chimes within a broader "blame the victim" culture. This should, perhaps, bring to mind the saying, "...there but for the grace of God, go I".

Poverty and social disadvantage is an issue that is of particular pertinence across our "hidden worlds". The beatings and extreme violence carried out against vulnerable young people which is a major feature of Katy Radford's chapter emerges directly from the working-class estates and an environment of socio-economic disadvantage. For this reason, Radford's contribution should be very broadly applicable well beyond the Northern Ireland context. In fact, anywhere that central government is weakened and rivalries within communities are strong, and powerful associations, criminal gangs or war lords and the like, struggle over an impoverished population for influence and a political voice.

Overall, the weight of evidence gathered here strongly suggests that the family is not fragmenting, but is indeed changing. The picture presented is not one of social decay, but of social change, and very often change for the better. However, this is hardly possible in social conditions in which the weight of adversity is overwhelming, especially where effective support mechanisms are not available. Poverty and social disadvantage provide entirely the wrong social context for families to tackle their problems.

By and large, there has been a gradual shift over time from an emphasis on discipline and correction towards a recognition that people thrive best in conditions of encouragement and support. Clearly, government policy sometimes falls short in this regard. Heavily distracted by the lobbying of very powerful interest groups intent on preserving the status quo, the government is in danger of lagging behind the changing attitudes and positive social renewal of family structures that are necessary to accommodate the rising diversity of family arrangements.

Furthermore, the widespread anxiety that the family is fragmenting, that things are getting worse and that substance abusers, criminals, an undisciplined and uncommitted youth, are among those to blame for this, is also played upon by powerful media interests intent on selling "bad news" and accustomed to playing on the public fears of marginalised and stigmatised social groups. However, this book informs us of the need for robust and effective support structures, emptied of all social structural impediments, so as to enable people to apply their own resources in their attempts to preserve their families, to overcome their difficulties, and to thrive.

All of the chapters in this volume remain loyal to the call by Wright Mills for a "sociological imagination". They each depict with great clarity families struggling against dilemmas and adversity in the contemporary moment and social structure – families struggling to negotiate their "private troubles" within the strictures imposed by contemporary "public issues". This volume is indeed an instructive and informative body of work that will provide a substantial resource to students of the family everywhere.

David Charles Ford

Reference

Wright Mills, C. (1959). *The Sociological Imagination*. Oxford: Oxford University Press.

WHY DON'T THEY MARRY? COMMITMENT AND COHABITATION IN 21st CENTURY BRITAIN[1]

Simon Duncan, Anne Barlow and Grace James

Introduction: Unmarried cohabitation as irrational behaviour?

Unmarried heterosexual cohabitation (henceforth "cohabitation") is both widely practised and accepted in Britain. The British Social Attitudes [BSA] (2000) survey shows that over a third of people under 35 who live with a partner are unmarried, and over 80% of this age group view cohabitation as "all right" (Barlow, Duncan, James & Park, 2001, p. 35). At this time, over a quarter of births were to cohabitants, and around 60% of this age group also thought this acceptable. Whilst older people practise cohabitation less (cohabitation is common for older people with a new partner after divorce), the majority are still accepting of it and even think it is a good idea before marriage. Similarly, there was little difference in the practice and acceptance of cohabitation by social class, except that it is more likely for the better off to get married when they have children. The average period spent in cohabitation is also becoming longer. Consequently, both the incidence of cohabitation and the numbers of children

---

[1] Since this chapter was originally written in 2005, Anne Barlow jointly conducted a 2006 British Social Attitudes Survey (BSAS) following up the issues emerging from the original 2000 BSAS cohabitation survey used here. See 'Cohabitation and the law: myths, money and the media' in A. Park et al. (eds.) *British Social Attitudes: the 24th Report*, London: Sage (2008 with C. Burgoyne, E. Clery and J. Smithson). See also A. Barlow, S. Duncan, G. James, and A. Park (2005) *Cohabitation, Marriage and the Law*, Oxford: Hart Publishing, for fuller treatment of many of the issues raised in this chapter. The chapter was delivered as a paper at Chester by Simon Duncan.

with unmarried but cohabiting parents are expected to increase substantially over coming decades. In this way, Britain seems to be moving towards a Scandinavian pattern where cohabitation is quite normal and where marriage is more of a lifestyle choice rather than an expected part of life.

At first sight all this seems like mass irrationality. This is because marriage in Britain gives partners substantial and automatic legal benefits which they do not possess as unmarried cohabitants. In brief, married spouses automatically acquire: rights to reasonable financial support from their partner; occupation rights in the matrimonial home; exemption from capital gains and inheritance tax for asset transfers between each other; access to financial support on divorce or separation; joint parental responsibility; better protection from domestic violence; succession into a partner's pension; and automatic entitlement into their estate on death, if no will has been made. It is not that cohabitants do not have any legal rights. In some situations, the law even treats cohabitants as equal to married spouses, notably in allocating means-tested benefits or tax credits (although even then the partner in receipt of benefit has no legal duty to share this income!). In other situations, the law does recognise the familial nature of cohabitation, but sees this as inferior to marriage (for example, in inheritance claims on a deceased partner's estate). In yet other circumstances, the law simply treats cohabitants, even long-standing ones with children, as complete strangers (as with pension payments and partner maintenance). For cohabitants, the law is confusing, complex, usually inferior, and hardly ever automatic (see Barlow, Duncan, James & Park, 2005). Those people, generally children and caring dependants, who are the most vulnerable in families, especially on breakdown or death, are particularly vulnerable as cohabiting family members.

There are legal remedies to which cohabitants can turn in tackling some of these disadvantages. That said, the BSA (2000) survey showed that only 14% of current cohabitants had changed or made wills, just 9% had made property agreements, and an even lower proportion of fathers, just 5%, had obtained parental responsibility agreements or orders (from 1 December 2003, unmarried fathers who jointly register the childbirth receive parental rights, although this is not automatic or retrospective). Most cohabitants remained in a vulnerable legal situation.

This paper will focus on whether cohabitants are acting irrationally in not getting married and, if they are not, what is the basis of their rationalities for not marrying? There are two major sources of new empirical evidence available to draw upon. These are, the nationally representative BSA survey undertaken in 2000, and 48 in-depth qualitative interviews of BSA respondents undertaken in 2001 (later supplemented by 25 interviews with members of minority ethnic groups).[2]

Explaining irrationality? Lack of knowledge and the common law marriage myth

At first sight, the "common law marriage myth" gives a plausible explanation of cohabitants' apparent irrationality

---

[2] Both were part of a Nuffield-funded project, 'Family restructuring, the common law marriage myth, and the need for legal realism'. The BSA sample took 3,101 respondents in England and Wales, and 1,663 in Scotland as part of the separate Scottish Social Attitudes Survey, 2000. The in-depth interviews comprised 48 current and former cohabitants drawn from the BSA sample in England and Wales, followed by two 'snowball' samples of 25 Afro-Caribbean and South Asian respondents who were inadequately represented in the other samples. See Barlow et al., (2005).

in not getting married. Certainly, the BSA (2000) survey shows that over half of all respondents (56%) believed that unmarried couples who lived together for some time "definitely" or "probably" had a common law marriage and are treated equally in law. Also, the survey shows that there is little difference in this proportion by social group or income. If marriage-like rights come automatically after a certain period of cohabitation, and/or after joint registration of a child, as many believe, then there is clearly much less need to go to the expense, practical trouble, and possible emotional conflict in getting married. Diane, who had been cohabiting for just a year and had one child, simply thought: "Well, what's the point of getting married because we're classed as though we're married - we're living together and if we do split up we still do what a married couple would do - split everything, kids, responsibility and everything."

Certainly, the British government gives this view some credence. Whilst the government "marriage-like" rights for same-sex cohabitants will be established through new civil partnership legislation, this benefit will be denied to heterosexual cohabitants because, the government argues, heterosexual couples can get married if they wish. It is just, government continues, that many people do not appreciate the true legal situation of unmarried cohabitation. Hence the Department for Constitutional Affairs began a publicity campaign in summer 2004, "to dispel the myth surrounding 'common law marriage'" (Department of Trade and Industry, Women and Equality Unit, 2003, para 3.6). However, as soon as we examine this "lack of knowledge" explanation further, we find that, at best, it can only provide a partial and superficial explanation of the rising tide of unmarried cohabitation.

The first problem for this explanation lies within the historical trends. When the practice of unmarried cohabitation is rapidly increasing, it seems reasonable to assume that belief in common law marriage is decreasing, or is at least stable. The evidence available (see Barlow et al., 2005) points towards a gradual decrease in the practice of unmarried cohabitation from the late eighteenth up to the mid-twentieth century, and, it can be assumed, a concomitant decrease in belief in the legal existence of common law marriage. Whilst there is no direct evidence of this, the spread of education, the deeper influence of mass media, and an increasing "legalisation" of society (for example, as people are more likely to consult lawyers in buying homes and other property, in getting divorced and so on) would surely suggest a reducing level of belief in common law marriage. The alternative explanation, which is to assume that people are becoming less legally aware over time and that this ignorance of the law is spreading among the well educated and rich just as much as the ill educated and poor, so that a belief in common law marriage is galloping apace to match the rising trend in cohabitation, is somewhat counter-intuitive.

A second major problem with the "ignorance" explanation lies in the longevity and enormity of this myth. Common law marriage was abolished by Act of Parliament in 1753. This being the case, how is it that such completely incorrect assumptions regarding the legality of common law marriage have survived for more than 250 years, a quarter of a millennium, for over half the British population? In contrast to this, by 2000 it was very widely known that homosexual relations for male adults were no longer illegal, a mere 33 years since the Sexual Offences Act of 1967. Similarly, less than 40 years after the 1969 Divorce Reform Act, most people know that simple breakdown of a marriage with separation is sufficient grounds for divorce. It is not the case that ordinary members of the public are experts on laws about sexual behaviour or divorce law, but rather that they are aware of the general direction and message framed within these laws. It seems unlikely, therefore, that they would prove to be so spectacularly and pervasively wrong in the related case of common law marriage. It might, perhaps, be expected that those who had not been cohabiting for very long, or who were ill educated, might show less knowledge. However, the BSA (2000) survey found that belief in common law marriage was common among all ages, social classes, and educational levels, and for single people, unmarried cohabitants (both short- and long-term) and married spouses alike. Both the longevity and pervasiveness of the common law marriage myth, and the enormous gulf between myth and law, point towards an alternative explanation; that the idea of common law marriage chimes in with people's everyday lived experience in some way. As the interviewees showed, belief, or non-belief, in common law marriage rests upon notions of social logic, fairness and morality. Beliefs about what the law does are conflated with beliefs about what the law *ought* to do. This may also help explain why the common law marriage myth is more pervasive and deeply held by people when issues concerning children are involved.

The behaviour of the third of the British population in 2000 who did *not* believe that common law marriage exists provides the *coup de grâce* for the "lack of knowledge" explanation for the prevalence of cohabitation. Certainly, there is little evidence for any increase in legal rationality in this group, compared to those who did believe the "myth". Indeed, there was no difference at all in the BSA (2000) survey between cohabitants in this non-believing group and cohabiting "myth-believers", in relation to the proportion who had taken out parental responsibility agreements/orders, or who had made property agreements. Whilst 15% of the non-believing group had made or changed a will as a result of cohabiting, compared to 9% of the "myth-believers", this is hardly a profound difference.

This lack of legal rationality was equally evident in the follow-up interviews. In most cases, people's perceptions of the legal consequences, whether accurate or inaccurate, had no impact on their decision to cohabit. This is equally apparent for those who do marry. Hibbs, Barton and Beswick (2001) found that 41% of their 1998/99 sample of 173 engaged respondents (three quarters of whom were already cohabiting) thought that marriage would not change the legal nature of their relationship; further, that as many as 37% saw no legal consequences of marriage for present or future children. Indeed, Hibbs et al. found only one respondent who cited "legal reasons" as a cause for marriage, and only 3% of their respondents admitted to any legal influence at all.

Similarly, in 2002, John Eekelaar and Mavis Maclean (2004) found only one out of 39 respondents who admitted to legal considerations as a reason for marrying. Most of our respondents, like those interviewed by Hibbs et al. (2001), were likely to view questions about legal measures with surprise, or even indignation. It was their view that marriage and living together had little to do with the law, and in any case they trusted and loved their partners. There was no need for a formal public document making their wish to have a union explicit, and it was the private promises between the partners that were regarded as the important thing. Duncan, a schoolteacher who had been cohabiting for 5 years, gives a nice summary of this consensus:

> ... there are some things that you are better off if you are married, but then that's not the final reason for getting married. What's the point of getting married if it's just to save money on your income tax

or your pensions or whatever else it might be ... They're not good
reasons in my view ...

This response perhaps indicates the key to why people
cohabit rather than marry. They see living together as an
emotional relationship, not an economic transaction.

Cohabitation and commitment

In political and media discourse, commitment to a
relationship is usually equated with marriage. Partners
who are committed to one another get married, unless (and
this is a recent addition to the argument) they are misled by
the common law marriage myth. In this discourse,
cohabitation is viewed as a second-rate family structure,
characterised as fragile, informal, and lacking commitment
(Ermisch, 2002; Morgan, 2000). This assumption is
supported by reference to statistical comparisons, where on
average married spouses are less likely to break up and
marriages last longer than cohabiting relationships. The
legal reflection of this assumption is illustrated by the
Family Law Act 1996. Cohabitation is defined as an
arrangement where: "a man and a woman who, although
not married to each other, are living together as husband
and wife" (s.62(1)); where judges should "have regard to
the fact that [cohabitants] have not given each other the
commitment involved in marriage" (s.41).

This is a picture that many cohabitants would not
recognise, still less agree with. Empirical studies, including
our own, routinely record expressions of commitment by
cohabitants that are little different from those of married
spouses. As C. Lewis, Papacosta and Warin (2002, p. 10)
point out, "The word used by the vast majority of
interviewees to describe cohabitation was 'commitment'":
(see also J. Lewis, 2001; Eekelaar & Maclean, 2004). In our

survey, for example, Susan favourably compared her current cohabiting union to a previous marriage:

> I don't see it as being married or not. What I do is compare my relationship, my and Mike's relationship, with the person I was with before, regardless of the fact that I was married to one and not to the other, and it's how happy I am and how the relationship's working, and I think that's much more important than the fact that one was a marriage and one isn't.

The implication that marriage was in some way evidence of more commitment evoked some heated responses from respondents. Indeed, some cohabitants claimed that the lack of a formal, legal union demands greater commitment on their part, and more attention to their partner and the relationship. This means cohabitation is the more ethically sound and honest relationship (C. Lewis et al., 2002). For Melanie, who had also been married before: "At least this way you know you're together because you love each other and you want to be together." As Jane Lewis (2001) reflects, "in this way it is unmarried cohabitants, not married spouses, who can claim the moral high ground".

The statistical evidence brought to support the "marriage equals commitment" assumption seems compelling at first sight, in that it draws upon what people actually do, rather than what they say. However sincerely expressed, the fact that cohabitants are more likely to break up and their unions last for less time appears to speak more about commitment than their happiness, aspirations or expectations. However, this argument often commits the statistical error of not comparing like with like.

First, the married population is on average older than the cohabiting population. Only around 20% of the married population is under 35, and just 2% under 25, compared to nearly 70% and 20% respectively of cohabitants. The age at which a partnership starts is one of the most powerful factors associated with subsequent breakdown. Younger unions, whether married or not, are less stable in both emotional and structural terms (Murphy, 1985; Thornes & Collard, 1979). If the cohabiting and married populations had the same age structures, this factor alone would substantially reduce differences in breakdown rates.

Secondly, cohabiting couples are less likely to have children, partly because of their younger age, and the presence of a child has been estimated to reduce breakdown rates by as much as 40% (Haskey, 1983; Murphy, 1985). Research also shows that there is very little difference in "relationship quality" between cohabitants and married spouses who have children or who want children (Brown & Booth, 1996).

Thirdly, cohabitation often follows marriage breakdown. "Post-separation cohabitation" has increasingly replaced remarriage, where the remarried are at a much higher risk of relationship breakdown.

Finally, the married population includes partners who find it difficult to separate because of external pressures, such as religion or family pressure. If we compared like with like, for example, young secular childless couples or older couples in a long-term union with children, there would probably be little difference between separation rates for cohabiting and married couples.

This is certainly what the evidence suggests. In the BSA (2000) survey, 23% of cohabitants had been together for over ten years. Although it is not possible or meaningful (just because so many marriages date from a time when cohabitation was uncommon) to give an average length of marriage, the median duration of those 40% of marriages currently ending in divorce is also about ten years. It is also important to note that the younger the age of partners at marriage, the higher the rates of breakdown (Haskey, 1983). The example of the "shotgun marriage" (where partners were virtually forced to marry after an unplanned pregnancy) is particularly telling. This social institution of the 1950s and 60s is now virtually extinct. By 2000, only 3% of marriages were preceded by pre-marital conceptions, compared to almost a quarter in 1970, and "shotgun marriages" were notorious for high rates of dysfunctionality and breakdown (Coombs & Zumeta, 1970; Thornes & Collard, 1979).

If we are to compare commitment between married and unmarried cohabiting partners, we need to define what it is and what makes it up. Jane Lewis (2001) refers to the distinction of three dimensions to commitment. These are:

1. Personal commitment to the partner, summed up as wanting the relationship to continue;
2. Moral-normative commitment, summed up as the feeling that the relationship ought to continue;
3. Structural commitment, summed up as the feeling that a relationship has to continue because of the investments made in the relationship (for example, housing, finance, job arrangements, children) and the costs of ending it.

As discussed above, many, if not most of the cohabitants display the first, more personal dimension to commitment. There may be some types of cohabitation where partners do not feel this commitment so completely: for example, following an unexpected pregnancy. Equally, there will be marriages where this same dimension is also weak. Arranged marriages, "shotgun" marriages, or those made for largely economic reasons, can provide examples. In these cases, it will be dimensions 2 and 3 that keep the partnership intact. Whilst structural commitment (dimension 3) is not normally felt or experienced until dimensions 1 and 2 are weak and thus the partnership is liable to break up, it is easy to show that most cohabitants will be as subject to this dimension as are the married spouses. Studies show that divisions of labour, leisure behaviour, the sharing of property and income, and joint responsibility for children, are virtually identical for married and cohabiting couples (J. Lewis, 2001; C. Lewis et al., 2002; Eekalaar & Maclean, 2004). Our own interviews confirmed this general consensus, indicating virtually identical outcomes if age is taken into account. Indeed, practices seem to vary much more by generation than by the form of the union. Similarly, the divide was much more focused between men and women than between cohabiting and married partners. If a lack of joint involvement in childcare and household chores is taken as an index of commitment to a relationship, then some married couples must be very uncommitted indeed!

It might be expected that cohabitants would differ more from married couples on the second dimension of commitment: moral-normative views that the relationship ought to continue. There is some evidence that this is sometimes the case. For a small sample of separated cohabitants with children, Charlie Lewis et al. (2002), found that some respondents saw cohabitation as offering greater freedom to monitor, re-evaluate and negotiate their relationships at any time. If people "grew apart", then relationships could more easily be ended. These same respondents thought of marriage as putting people under pressure to stay together, sometimes seen negatively in terms of preventing self-development and honesty, but sometimes seen as positive because of the feeling that important relationships "ought to continue". In contrast, Jane Lewis (2001), using a small sample of long-established partnerships with children, found that the association between obligation and marriage was restricted to an older generation married in the 1950s and 60s. Their own children, aged between 27 and 50, whether married or cohabiting, all believed that commitment came from within, from love of the other person and their children, rather than any externally prescribed moral code. The only difference between cohabitants and married spouses for this group concerned the wider presentation of their commitment. Cohabitants saw their commitment as private, whereas those who had married (often after long-term cohabitation) felt the need to make a public commitment. For the cohabitants, commitment was private in two senses. First, it was theirs alone and did not involve state, church, community or kin; and secondly, it eschewed any public ceremony.

For the married couples, public commitment seemed to be most important for relatives and kin, especially the parents, who then knew where the relationship stood and how they should behave as a result. This is echoed by Eekalaar and Maclean's (2004) discovery that marriage was often undertaken as a matter of "conformity", and was particularly aimed at pleasing relatives. However, the more private commitment made by cohabitants does not necessarily mean it is weaker or less committed. Indeed, all of Jane Lewis's sample acknowledged the importance of the fact that they had made a commitment. Our own interviews of cohabitants revealed a similar response: that marriage was basically about making a commitment public, although sometimes it was seen negatively as just showing off or keeping up with the Joneses. Nonetheless, the basis for their partnership was a strong private commitment to another person.

It is clear that many unmarried cohabitants see themselves as being just as committed to their partners as married people and furthermore, when comparing like with like, that their behaviour seems to bear this out. Whilst there are different types of cohabitation and

31

marriage, and each may show a range of commitment, the evidence does not support the "official" assumption that cohabitation necessarily means less or contingent commitment. As Jane Lewis (2001) concluded, the crucial thing for the majority is the existence of commitment, rather than whether it is manifested as marriage or unmarried cohabitation. This means, in turn, that, by and large, cohabiting partners do not avoid marriage because of low levels of commitment.

This conclusion returns us to the original problem, however. If cohabiting partners are mostly just as committed as married spouses, and if they can gain substantial legal benefits and potential economic gains from marriage, then why do they not marry? In fact, the problem is compounded as, rather than seeing partners as selfish individuals, we can now see them as committed and caring individuals who presumably would like their partners and children to have the full protection of the law. Certainly, as the BSA (2000) survey showed, a large majority thinks that the legal benefits of marriage should be extended to cohabitants. The following section will examine how cohabiting partners themselves explain why they end up cohabiting, rather than getting married.

The reasons for cohabitation

The argument so far has revealed alternative moralities and rationalities, through which large numbers of people in Britain see cohabitation as an adequate way of conducting committed relationships with other adults and of bringing up children. Further consideration of this situation can be undertaken through an analysis of the reasons given by cohabitants, in the interviews, to explain why they were cohabiting, rather than being married. This analysis follows Prinz (1995) who distinguishes between:

1. Cohabitation as a prelude to marriage;
2. Cohabitation as a variety of marriage;
3. Cohabitation as an alternative to marriage.

Cohabitation as a prelude to marriage

Cohabitation has often been viewed as a simple prelude to marriage. Couples are simply trying out living together with marriage in mind. Successful unions are transformed into a legal and formal marriage, and other partnerships just break up. Whilst couples will have a level of commitment to one another, this is not the same as a long-term commitment. Consequent to this view, there would be little need, and little desire, for the extension of marriage-like legal rights to cohabitants.

It is indeed the case that it is now both statistically normal, and a socially expected norm, that couples will start by living together through unmarried cohabitation. However, it is important here to distinguish between a general, but vague, expectation that marriage might occur at some unspecified point in the future, and a more conscious trial marriage. The concern here is with living together as a conscious preparation for marriage.

Many of our interviewees did indeed acknowledge this sort of cohabitation. Pamela, who married during the course of the research, put this most vividly:

> It's like going to buy a car. You don't go and buy a car without test-driving it, would you, at the end of the day? That's the way I've felt. Live together, test each other out first, and you feel like you've done the hard work.

Gail, a nursery nurse with one daughter, expanded on what the trial consisted of:

> How can you know that you're going to like living with this person until you've lived with them. Everybody's got faults and they don't

33

come out till you're living with them, so if you've gone out and got married and then gone to live with them it must be a big culture shock....

As the BSA (2000) survey shows, this view of the advantages of living together before marriage is widespread. However, as this survey also shows, this "trial" period is often quite a long one. The mean duration of cohabitation was six and a half years, and only 20% of current cohabitants had been living together for less than a year. In other words, most cohabitants live together for much longer than any reasonable trial period. Partners would presumably have discovered most of each other's hidden faults after a year or so of "test-driving". For example, Pamela and Gail, quoted above in expounding the benefits of cohabiting as trial marriage, had in fact both been cohabitants for eight years at the time of the interview. In such cases, cohabitation has progressed beyond a "trial" to a committed long-term relationship. Formal marriage may remain an expectation, but is now just one part of the progression of the partnership, rather than a means of establishing and defining it.

Several interviewees described this evolutionary process, as a relationship progressed from initial dating to committed, long-term co-residence. Marriage was more an incidental in this progress, rather than a defining marker. By the same token, it is important to remember that the reasons for entering a relationship are not necessarily the reasons why people stay in a relationship. Thus, some of our interviewees gave striking retrospective accounts of the various stages through which their partnerships had progressed. Importantly, although marriage had been considered by some at particular times in this journey, it was not seen as necessary to this progression.

The evolution of cohabitation from trial marriage into a "variety of marriage" also fits with the statistical evidence of union formation and dissolution. If cohabitation was simply used as a preparation for marriage, then the number of marriages and the cohabiting rate should remain roughly constant. Neither of these propositions is true. It appears that "trial" marriage often develops into long-term cohabitation.

Cohabitation as an alternative to marriage

Cohabitation has sometimes been interpreted as an alternative to marriage. For most of our interviewees, this was not the case. Living together unmarried was perceived rather as a long-term prelude to marriage, or as a variety of marriage. However, a significant minority of our BSA (2000) qualitative interview respondents (16 out of 48) did see cohabitation as an alternative to marriage, in the sense that they were opposed to marriage, even though they wanted to live with and commit to a partner.

There were two main reasons for using cohabitation as an alternative to marriage. The first was a desire to avoid male control. For some interviewees, this reflected a long-term principle, when marriage was seen as a patriarchal institution. Cohabitation offered the better way to commit to a partner in an egalitarian way, free of externally imposed rules. For others, being married in the past had encouraged this "political" view of marriage. Their experiences had identified marriage as a form of male control. The second, and overlapping, reason for avoiding marriage was disillusion with marriage as an effective institution. In these cases, marriage was seen as a failing or dangerous institution, in which there was a strong possibility of breakdown and where the costs of this were high. This viewpoint had often been confirmed by close or personal experience. It is this perception of high costs and likely breakdown that may help to explain why a high proportion of cohabitants, up to a third according to John Haskey (2001), are either divorced or separated from spouses.

Cohabitation as a variety of marriage

In contrast to the above, most of our cohabiting interviewees saw themselves as "good as married". They may have begun to live together as a "trial", or because of an unexpected pregnancy or housing problems, but that was some time ago and their relationship had now progressed to a long-term, committed partnership. Others had become "married" in this sense straight away. As Chris, who had been cohabiting for six years and had two daughters, explained: "We were just courting, and decided we wanted to be more serious. Children were on the agenda straight away, so we talked about it and decided to have the children straight away." This was no principled alternative to marriage, but rather, because cohabiting as if married was an alternative to remaining single. Angela, cohabiting for 13 years with one son, elaborated: "We'd been together for about three years before we moved in together. I can't really remember how it came about but ... I wanted more commitment and he said: 'Right, we'll live together'."

Jane Lewis (2001) found much the same viewpoint within her small sample of long-established partners with children. Most saw themselves as "good as married" and could see little point in getting married now, even when they did not reject marriage as an institution. Hence, most interviewed cohabitants in our own sample, and in Lewis's, expressed and practised levels of commitment in the same ways as demographically similar married couples. Their union may not have been formalised by law, but for them this was a side issue.

36

This experience of cohabitation as a variety of marriage can be described as a type of "lived law". This concept, taken from anthropological research on social behaviour in sub-Saharan Africa (Hodgson, 2000; Odgaard, 2002), refers to the situation where peoples' everyday behaviour is governed by informal, but socially and locally embedded, codes of behaviour. These codes may ignore or even contradict the formal state legal code which, in contrast, has little social embedding. Thus, in Britain, the idea of common law marriage is validated by day-to-day practice in everyday life. Heterosexual cohabitants, certainly those with children and/or some length of co-residence, are commonly treated as "man and wife". Socially, they are usually treated as an exclusive couple, and the female partner is often referred to as "Mrs". Similarly, the cohabitants will often present themselves in an equivalent way, even at times referring to their "in-laws". In maternity wards, doctors' surgeries, school meetings, work parties and social gatherings throughout the land, cohabitants will receive affirmation of married status. Or, increasingly, married spouses will be treated as cohabitants by inclusion in the more universal category of "partner". Reflecting this public discourse, institutions come to use common law marriage as a definitional category. Their treatment of customers in working out insurance premiums, for example, may differ as a result. Such official definitions can promote a quite powerful validation of the "myth", because many people will have day-to-day experience of this parity. Again, this as an area in which periodic experience will validate the "myth". This "lived law" then comes full circle when state bodies use "common law marriage" as a social category. Government, and hence the law, treats unmarried cohabitants as husband and wife in applying eligibility rules about joint income and expenditures. As a result, state bodies have come up with various definitions of cohabitation, mostly based upon evidence of shared living arrangements, a sexual relationship, stability, financial support, the presence of children, and public acknowledgement (Davies, 1999). These definitions are then employed to equate cohabiting couples with married couples. Everyday social and institutional practice treats longer-term cohabitants, especially those with children, just like married couples.

All this amounts to what we might call "do-it-yourself" marriage. More grandly, to adapt from Bourdieu, this common type of cohabitation is a form of "institutional bricolage" (Cleaver, 2002). People have taken existing institutional forms, in this case formal marriage and the lived law of "living together as if married" (as the Inland Revenue puts it), combined them, and developed their own variety of marriage. They have responded to change by drawing on and adapting existing norms. This is partly to conserve cognitive and social energy. It is far harder to forge completely new institutions, as the pioneers of 1970s communes can testify. In so doing, people confer the new arrangements of "common law marriage" with the legitimacy of tradition, and this therefore becomes part of "the right way of doing things". As we have seen, this do-it-yourself marriage does not exclude formal marriage, and partners are not opposed to legal marriage. Indeed, why should they be, when they perceive themselves to be as good as married? Rather, formal marriage is often seen more as an expectation, sometimes a rather vague and ideal expectation, for some future date. People do not marry because they are socially, in terms of lived law, and privately, in terms of commitment, as good as married already.

Why Don't They Marry?

So - What is marriage for?

If cohabiting partners can be "as good as married", then why bother with formal marriage at all, even as a vague expectation? Clearly, for some, partnership means public commitment, which means marriage. The concern here, however, is with the large group who see little difference between formal marriage and "lived law" cohabitation as marriage, but are not particularly opposed to marriage. For some respondents, especially those who did not believe in common law marriage, there were "formal" legal reasons for marriage. A few respondents who were contemplating marriage pointed to the ability to tidy up financial arrangements through legal marriage. Others cited the "name change myth", particularly if there were children involved. Marriage would secure the same name for all members of the family. In fact, female name changing upon marriage is not a legal requirement, but rather a powerful tradition. Neither is it illegal to take on your partner's name without marriage, or to choose a combined surname for children. This belief appears as the converse to the common law marriage myth.

It is the wedding which is the obvious social difference between official and "do-it-yourself" marriage, and the major reason for wanting marriage, as expressed by our sample, either as a vague expectation or as a practical plan, was for public performance and display. As most cohabitants saw themselves as "good as married", then there was no need for a cheap and easy register office marriage to mark their personal commitment. Rather, the respondents wanted a "proper wedding" to show this publicly. Caroline explained:

> Probably somewhere in beautiful grounds, beautiful gardens, all outside, beautiful cars or horse-drawn carriage - really spend a few grand on it and have a really fantastic day for him as well as for her.

Fragmenting Family?

We could go to the Register Office up the road tomorrow if we wanted!

To see the wedding as public display is quite logical. After all, it is a public occasion. There are, however, two crucial differences to earlier practice. The first one refers to the expense involved. Display does not only mean marriage in public, but conspicuous consumption. Secondly, when partners often see themselves as already as good as married, marriage itself becomes reduced to the "proper wedding". This is reminiscent of Tony Giddens's description of marriage as a "shell institution" (Giddens, 1999) and of Ulrich Beck's notion of social institutions as "zombie categories" which are "dead and still alive" (Beck, 2002, p. 203). In this view, the structural reasons which support a particular institution are fatally weakened and enormous changes have taken place in what actually happens, although the façade is seemingly unchanged. In this case, marriage is no longer socially expected for partnership and childbearing, and relations within marriage are conducted in quite different ways than before. The institution itself survives, although emptied of its former social content, and is now used for something quite different from before.

So, if a "proper wedding" is about display, what is this display about and what is being shown to friends and relatives? We might imagine that one motive is the desire to show personal commitment through public performance. In practice, this seemed to be linked to a desire to show social success. Marriage is no longer a rite of passage into adulthood, as in the 1950s and 60s, but rather a rite of passage into the ranks of the socially successful. Many of our respondents were less circumspect, and simply saw marriage as a means of showing off. Sharon, cohabiting for seven years with three children, had no thoughts of marriage and speculated: "I suppose people try and outdo each other. I suppose it's keeping up with the Joneses. If your friends get married and have a big white wedding, then you probably want one bigger and better. Philip, a JP shortly to be married, was more caustic:

> I feel that a young bride likes to have a big day to show off to her friends, her family and everybody else. "Look, it's me, I'm getting married, we're going to spend £15,000- £20,000" - which is quite the norm now - "Look at me, look at us".

Pamela, recently married, but previously cohabiting for eight years with her husband to be, explained why showing off was so important, and why this meant material expense to work well:

> I think it's ever so important today, because it's such a materialistic world. Everybody is trying to outdo everybody on everything. For example, my wedding dress was £700 ... and I thought that was lot of money - a friend of mine who got married the other month, her dress was £2,500 and it was beautiful and everything, but it's like everybody's trying to outdo everybody.

The wedding as public display, to be effective, costs a lot of money. This commodification of marriage as another consumer good, albeit one which is particularly useful in establishing social status, has certain economic consequences. Some people will not be able to afford the good and, for everyone, the good will be subject to opportunity costs. We found this to be a telling factor in the minds of many respondents (as did Eekelaar & Maclean, 2004). Sharon was therefore inclined to give formal marriage a miss: "Expense is a major factor. It's not cheap to get married ... if we had the sort of money to get married, I'd rather take the children on holiday personally or he'd rather have a new car ...". Gail simply ranked marriage beneath other, more attractive, acquisitions:

It's a case of we're looking now for a conservatory for the house and that's going to cost a lot more money. We want to start going on holidays and that's costing money. He says, "What would you rather have?": a new car, we got a new car last year. It's "What would you rather have, a new car or a wedding?" and now it's a conservatory.

For these cohabitants, who saw themselves as being as good as married, the legal side of getting married formally, just like the legal side of not being married, remained peripheral. The church or civil registration was just another part of the ritual on which to hang the public display of a "proper marriage". They had no objections to marriage and felt that the same norms were applicable to both cohabitation and marriage, and even intended to marry formally eventually. This sort of cohabitation is a "do-it-yourself" variety of marriage.

Discussion – Virtual and real families in policy making

Cohabitants seem to show just as much commitment to their partnerships, when comparing like with like, as married people do. Some cohabitants are less committed than others, but the same goes for married people. Some sort of dramatic spread in lack of commitment, therefore, cannot explain the increasing levels of cohabitation in Britain. Nor is ignorance of the law, in the form of widespread belief in the common law marriage myth, a satisfactory explanation for increasing cohabitation.

Rather, the research shows that large numbers of people in Britain perceive and experience cohabitation as a type of marriage. First, the majority now experience cohabitation as a prelude to marriage. However, "marriage" in this case does not necessarily mean formal, legally registered marriage. Increasingly, longer-term cohabitation is seen as a variety of marriage and such cohabitants are "as good as married". Even many of the minority who are opposed to marriage, either for reasons of principle or because of practical disillusionment, are in effect practising a variety of marriage. Cohabitation is experienced as an adequate way of conducting committed relationships with other adults and of bringing up children. Cohabitants are not acting irrationally, therefore, although many are left in a less secure legal position than married spouses. Nor should the rapid changes occurring in formal marriage itself be overlooked, where re-evaluation of the partnership is increasingly taken for granted and, consequently, where divorce has become a functional necessity and almost a part of the life course. It is perhaps more accurate to say that marriage is a variety of cohabitation. Both cohabitants and married spouses are attempting to work out how to combine personal freedom with commitment to others. In this way, it is quite wrong to see the statistical decrease in marriage and the rise in unmarried cohabitation as leading to or reflecting the "breakdown of the family".

Unfortunately, much legal policy and discourse has not gone inside the black boxes. In focusing on outward distinctions in the legal form of families, on cohabitation versus marriage, this debate has neglected what families actually do. The similarities between cohabitation and marriage have thereby been missed. In this way, policy has instead become fixated on attributing family dysfunctionality by form, where cohabitation is seen as the inferior type of partnership. Rather, policy should focus on how partners can best exercise care and commitment towards each other and their children.

References

Barlow, A., Duncan, S., James, G., and Park, A. (2001). Just a piece of paper?: Marriage and cohabitation. In A. Park, J. Curtice, K. Thomson, L. Jarvis, and C. Bromley (Eds.), *British social attitudes: The 18th report: Public policy, social ties* (pp. 29-57). London: Sage.

Barlow, A., Duncan, S., James, G., and Park, A. (2005). *Cohabitation, marriage and the law: Social change and legal reform in the 21st century.* Oxford: Hart.

Beck, U. (2002). Zombie categories: interview with Ulrich Beck, conducted by J. Rutherford. In U. Beck and E. Beck-Gernsheim, *Individualization: Institutionalized individualism and its social and political consequences* (pp. 202-213). London: Sage.

Brown, S., & A. Booth. (1996). Cohabitation versus marriage: A comparison of relationship quality. *Journal of Marriage and the Family, 58,* 668-678.

Cleaver, F. (2002). Reinventing institutions; Bricolage and the social embeddedness of natural resource management. *The European Journal of Development Research, 14* (2), 11-30.

Coombs, L. C., and Zumeta, Z. (1970). Correlates of marital dissolution in a prospective fertility study: A research note. *Social Problems, 18,* 92-102.

Davies, C. (1999). The definition of cohabitation. *Solicitors Family Law Association Review, 79,* 15-16.

Department of Trade and Industry, Women and Equality Unit. (2003). *Responses to civil partnership: A framework for the legal recognition of same-sex couples,* London: Department of Trade and Industry.

Eekelaar, J., and Maclean, M. (2004). Marriage and the moral bases of personal relationships. *Journal of Law and Society, 31,* 510-538.

Ermisch, J. (2002). *Trying again: Repartnering after dissolution of a union.* Colchester: University of Essex, Institute for Social and Economic Research.

Giddens, A. (1999). *Runaway world: How globalisation is shaping our lives.* London: Profile.

Haskey, J. (1983). Marital status before marriage and age at marriage: Their influence on the chance of divorce. *Population Trends, 32,* 4-14.

Haskey, J. (2001). Cohabitation in Great Britain: Past, present and future trends – and attitudes. *Population Trends, 103,* 4-25.

Hibbs, M., Barton, C., and Beswick, J. (2001). Why marry?: Perceptions of the affianced. *Family Law, 31,* 197-207.

Hodgson, D. (2000). My daughter belongs to the government now: Marriage, Maasai and the Tanzanian state. In C. Creighton and C. K. Omori (Eds.), *Gender, family and work in Tanzania.* Aldershot: Ashgate.

Home Office (1998) *Supporting families: A consultative document,* London: The Stationery Office.

Laurie, H. and Gershuny, J. (2000). 'Couples, work and money'. In Berthoud, R. and Gershuny, J. (Eds.), *Seven years in the lives of British households.* Bristol: Policy Press.

Lewis, C., Papacosta, A., and Warin, J. (2002). *Cohabitation, separation and fatherhood.* York: Joseph Rowntree Foundation.

Lewis, J. (2001). *The end of marriage?: Individualism and intimate relationships.* Cheltenham: Elgar.

Morgan, P. (2000). *Marriage-lite: The rise of cohabitation and its consequences.* London: Institute for the Study of Civil Society.

Murphy, M. (1985). Demographic and socio-economic influences on recent British marital breakdown patterns. *Population Studies, 39,* 441-460.

Odgaard, R. (2002). Scrambling for land in Tanzania: Processes of formalisation and legitimisation of land rights. *The European Journal of Development Research, 14,* 71-88.

Prinz, C. (1995). *Cohabiting, married or single: Portraying, analyzing, and modeling new living arrangements in the changing societies of Europe.* Aldershot: Avebury.

Smart, C., & Stevens, P. (2000). *Cohabitation breakdown,* London and York: Family Policy Studies Centre/Joseph Rowntree Foundation.

Thornes, B., & Collard, J. (1979). *Who divorces?* London: Routledge and Kegan Paul.

UK Statutes. (1967). *Sexual Offences Act: Elizabeth II, 1967, Chapter 60.* London: HMSO.

UK Statutes. (1969). *Divorce Reform Act: Elizabeth II, 1969, Chapter 55.* London: HMSO.

UK Statutes. (1996). *Family Law Act: Elizabeth II, 1966, Chapter 27.* London: HMSO.

FRAGMENTING FAMILIES: THE DEVASTATING LEGACY OF DOMESTIC VIOLENCE [1]

Gill Hague

Fragmenting families are all around us. An important issue in the analysis of the family, and of its potential for fragmenting, is the prevalence and nature of domestic violence within it. Abuse and fragmentation tend to go hand in hand. We are all, of course, familiar with the view of the family as a haven in a heartless world, a safe place to which we can retreat when the going gets tough and it seems that the world is against us (Lasch, 1995). However, for women and their children who experience domestic violence, and for some men, the family is anything but safe. In fact, it can be the most dangerous place.

Many analyses have emphasised the multiple changing forms that families take in the modern world and have explored power relations between family members and the impact of gender and age differences upon family relationships (Barrett & McIntosh, 1982; Muncie, Cochrane, Dallos & Wetherell, 1995; Demo, Allen & Fine, 2000). Whether you are a child or an adult, young or old, and whether you are male or female, can be key to how you experience family life. Power and patterns of domination and control between family members are also critical to the understanding of domestic violence. The impact of these may differ across different types of family structure, from extended to nuclear to single parent families, and there are also many variations in how families function according to culture and ethnicity. A claim that there is only one type of

---

[1] This chapter draws particularly on the third edition of *Domestic Violence: Action for Change,* by the author and Ellen Malos.

family cannot be substantiated. Black feminists have particularly cautioned others not to generalise, stating that white feminists and policy-makers need to beware of making assumptions about black families (Amos & Parmar, 1984, p. 11).

All of these differences, nuances and complexities need to be taken into account then when we start to think about domestic abuse in families. While it is important to avoid over-generalisation, domestic violence is so common and widespread that it crosses all types of families. In this chapter, the impact of domestic violence on family life in the UK will be discussed, including a review of definitions of domestic violence, its extent and impact, and policy and activist responses and explanations. Throughout, diversity, difference and variations according to culture, disability, social class and other factors that challenge claims to universality will be considered.

Activism against domestic violence

In recent decades in the UK, domestic violence has become an important issue within the social and caring services, the media, the criminal justice system, and the social sciences. The growing significance of the issue is largely because of the efforts of national and international activists within a wide-ranging movement against gender violence.

In this country, the advent of the women's movement in the 1970s and activism, backed up by research and service development, has transformed both our understandings of domestic violence in families and the practice of many agencies and services (see, for example, Dobash & Dobash, 1992; Hague & Malos, 2005). Women's Aid, the national domestic violence charity and activist body, co-ordinates refuges and other domestic violence services (see http://www.womensaid.org.uk), leading the way and working with a variety of other women's organisations and campaigning bodies. As a direct consequence of the activist effort, there is now an awareness of domestic violence that is very different from that of the past, when it was widely regarded as a regrettable, but "normal", phenomenon.

During the last thirty years, activists within the movement against domestic abuse have campaigned vigorously, sustained by a vision of women growing collectively more powerful and of an end to family violence. Largely as a result of these activities, we now hear about domestic violence frequently. The issue is discussed on radio and television, there is some legal and police protection against it, and there are services available to victims of domestic violence. This is in marked contrast to the situation prior to the 1970s, when there was silence on the issue and women experiencing violence in the home had virtually no one to turn to for help (Hague & Wilson, 1996).

Who experiences domestic violence?: Definitions and incidence

Domestic abuse against women is a global phenomenon. It occurs to a greater or lesser extent (and with only very few reliably documented exceptions) in almost all countries, societies, cultures, ethnic groups and communities, and it has done so throughout time, as far as anyone can tell. Such a wide-ranging and embedded human behaviour inevitably gives rise to varying interpretations and understandings. Therefore, it is important to document precisely what is currently meant by the term "domestic violence" in the UK.

Violence in the family takes many forms and includes the abuse of elders and children. However, the term "domestic violence" generally denotes something more specific. It is usually regarded as violence between adults who are (or have been) in an intimate or family relationship with each other, most often a sexual relationship between a woman and a man. Research suggests that about 90% of domestic violence is perpetrated by men against women. Evidence from research, from police records and crime statistics, and more broadly from history, culture, literature and our own lived experience, all point to the fact that domestic violence is overwhelmingly committed by men against women - women with whom they often share the most intimate of relationships and who they may profess to love (Hague & Malos, 2005). It is important, however, to acknowledge that female violence against men also exists, and these victims deserve services, help and support.

Although potentially equally devastating, there is some evidence to suggest that women's violence towards men is likely to be less serious and result in fewer injuries, perhaps because it can be more easily deflected by the man, and in many cases (although not all) is used solely as a means of self-defence. Domestic violence may also occur in lesbian and gay relationships, and this type of abuse has become a contemporary research focus (Donovan & Hester, 2008).

In general, the term "domestic violence" (and the use of the word "domestic" in particular) is rather confusing and not always used consistently. It could well refer to any violence that happens in the domestic environment, even when there is no personal relationship. In consequence, many have questioned its usefulness, and some activists prefer terms like "male violence against women in the home" or "the assault of women by known men". Such phrases as these locate the violence much more precisely, although they hardly slip easily from the tongue or pen. Of course, domestic violence does not only occur inside the home, or between current sexual partners. For example, the domestic abuse of women can be perpetrated by ex-partners or ex-husbands, or by men with whom they have sexual relations, but no joint living arrangements.

Domestic violence occurs between adults, but many definitions also acknowledge impacts on the children in the family. The children of women experiencing domestic violence are very often negatively affected by witnessing or living with such violence, and may be abused themselves. In such cases, domestic violence and child abuse may overlap (Hague & Malos, 2005; Hester, Pearson & Harwin, 2007).

The UK government defines domestic violence as:

> Any violence between current and former partners in an intimate relationship, wherever the violence occurs. The violence may include physical, sexual, emotional and financial abuse. Domestic violence occurs across society regardless of age, gender, race, sexuality, wealth and geography. (Home Office, 2005)

This, and most other definitions, emphasise that domestic violence includes physical, sexual, emotional/ psychological and economic abuse, and that different types of violence often occur in combination. Coercive control over the victim now features in many of these definitions (see Stark, 2007).

On a global scale, domestic violence is a significant cause of death and disability. World Health Organization research estimates that between one in three and one in five women worldwide experience gender violence across a lifetime (Garcia-Moreno, Jansen, Ellsberg, Heise & Watts, 2005). The devastating legacy of violence for women in their intimate relationships includes the shocking but related statistic of between 60 million and 100 million adult women missing from the world due to female infanticide and femicide (UNICEF, 1997). About two women are killed in domestic violence incidents every week in the UK.

This represents over half of murders of females: only 7-8% of killings of males are committed by intimate partners.

However, it is difficult to find out exactly how much domestic abuse occurs, owing to under-reporting and traditional silence about the issue. In 1998, Betsy Stanko conducted a study in the London Borough of Hackney and found a figure of one in nine women reporting domestic violence at any one time (Stanko, Crisp, Hale & Lucraft, 1998). Women's Aid has estimated that about one in ten women are likely to be experiencing domestic violence at any one time, and about one in four women may on occasion, over a life time, experience violence in their sexual relationships with men (http//:www.womensaid.org.uk). For example, ten separate studies into the prevalence of domestic violence were compared in a Council of Europe study which found that one in four women experienced domestic violence in their lives, and 6 to 10% in a single year (Hague & Malos, 2005). Cases of very severe, repeated and systematic violence are less common, but it has been estimated that this type of violence occurs in at least five out of a hundred marriages in the UK (Hague & Malos, 2005).

There have been few large-scale random studies of domestic violence, and none to date in the UK, although research is currently anticipated. The British Crime Survey now contains a self-completion questionnaire including questions on domestic violence, sexual assault and stalking (Walby & Allen, 2004). Whilst self-reporting questionnaires of this type may not provide a reliable estimate, as many people will discard them, the statistics for 2004 suggested that 13% of women and 9% of men had experienced domestic abuse, 45% of women could recall experiencing sexual assault, and approximately one-third of women victims had previously told no one else (Walby & Allen, 2004, pp. vii, x, vi).

What are the effects of domestic violence?: The impacts on women and children

Domestic violence in the family has very varied effects and levels of impact on women victims, which can range from the relatively mild through to the extreme. These include murder and attempted murder, damaged physical health, maiming, women being disabled, sexual damage and mutilation, broken bones, black eyes, pushing, shoving, slapping, mental health difficulties, depression, suicide and suicide attempts, anxiety, lowered self-esteem, and feelings of self-blame and worthlessness (Hague & Malos, 2005; Hester, Pearson & Harwin, 2007). In the UK, most domestic violence professionals argue that there is no one set of specific symptoms. Many are also resistant to discourses which talk about domestic violence in relation to post-traumatic stress disorder or battered women's syndrome (see Walker [1984] for a discussion of this syndrome, which is much used in the USA). However, whether or not a specific condition is "named", the damage that is done should not be underestimated and the range of injuries that women suffer, or are threatened with, is enormous.

Thus, we can see that the physical violence that women experience can comprise many types of assault, attack and injury. Commonly, it starts with a single slap or blow, followed by disbelief and shock on both sides and by commitments from the man that it will never be repeated. Sadly, after it has happened, it is rare for it not to happen again. Researchers across the disciplinary spectrum agree that domestic violence is rarely a one-off event. There may be long gaps with no violence, but men who have acted violently towards their wife, partner or lover tend to do so again, and then again. It is not unusual for women to endure many years of attacks without seeking or receiving any help from anybody.

Some women experience violence that results in hospitalisation and the need for medical treatment and care. In other cases, the injuries may not show. Some violent men are very skilled at inflicting violence on their partners that is not visible to the outside world. Violence may happen particularly frequently during pregnancy or in a post-separation period after a woman has tried to leave.

Sexual violence in intimate relationships within families is also distressingly common. Many domestic violence activists have used the idea of a continuum of male sexual mistreatment against women that links day-to-day harassment to severe assault, as part of the same broad spectrum (Kelly, 1988). Thus, the continuum includes the whole upsetting sweep of women's experiences of sexual violence, from "acceptable" sexual domination by men towards women, through to sexual assault and rape. The ultimate form of sexual violence is the murder and sexual mutilation of girls and women by male family members. However, Kelly suggests that, in general, it is not useful to think of the continuum as being graded in severity. A whole spectrum of harassment, degradation and coerced sexual activity is encompassed, including the use of pornography, for example, in the forced acting out of violent sexual fantasies. Within this context, it is to be greatly welcomed that rape in marriage was made a crime in the UK in the early 1990s.

The concept of domestic violence that focuses upon women's own experience of sexual violence, and on their feelings about what has happened to them, can be contentious. Women's activists have pointed out that society does not always want to hear what women have to say about this subject, and some men seem to act as if they have a vested interest in keeping definitions of sexual violence in the family as narrow as possible. It is vital that women continue to speak out, to tell their stories. However, naming and renaming, living and reliving the experience of sexual violence are not simple or easy processes. There may be no words for the pain and the shame. Some women may block these traumatic events out of their conscious memories, sometimes for many years, especially if the experiences occurred in childhood. Also, women and girls are frequently not believed. Even today, all too often they are instead blamed for the sexual violence that they have experienced (Hague & Malos, 2005).

Emotional or psychological abuse often accompanies physical abuse, frequently sapping the victim's self-confidence and sense of self-worth. Emotional abuse includes intimidating and threatening behaviour, as well as degradation and humiliation. Examples include being persistently insulted, or subjected continually to intimidation or verbal aggression. Psychological abuse can be financial (being denied money for children's food, for example). It can also be related to possessiveness and sexual jealousy.

Physical abuse is often accompanied by emotional and psychological abuse, and sexual violence runs through the lives of many who experience the other forms of abuse. The three forms of abuse are often interlinked, so that physical violence is one aspect of domestic violence and not necessarily the main one. In fact, some women say that the other types of abuse that they have experienced have been worse than the physical assaults. Women often experience several different kinds of abuse in combination.

The impact on the children of families in which there is domestic violence may lead to aggression, withdrawal, depression, suicide, running away, hiding, loss of confidence and self-worth, school and behavioural problems and bed-wetting (Mullender & Morley, 1994;

Hester, Pearson & Harwin, 2007). These can be severe and long-term, although they may well be hidden by the children concerned. They can also vary across cultural and ethnic heritages (Mullender et al., 2002; Mullender, 2004).

The children of women who have suffered violence have frequently been involved in the incidents experienced by their mothers. They may have tried to intervene, and may have been hurt themselves. They may also have been either physically or sexually abused independently. The degree of interrelatedness between domestic violence and child abuse has been studied by a variety of researchers. These studies show a varying degree of connection between the two, occurring together in somewhere between 30% and 60% of cases (Kelly, 1994; Hester, Pearson & Harwin, 2007). Of course, domestic violence against women is a different phenomenon from child abuse, with quite separate and distinct gender and power dynamics. It is not helpful to muddle the two. Many men who abuse their wives or partners would never deliberately harm their children. Nevertheless, the number of men who do abuse both their wives or partners and their children is disturbingly high, and an awareness of this possibility could be helpful in both domestic violence and in child protection cases.

Recent research has identified the remarkable coping strategies that some children use in dealing with domestic violence between their parents. Children are social actors in their own world, and often wish to talk about, and to be involved in working out solutions to domestic violence in the family when their involvement can be conducted safely. However, both professionals and parents very rarely ask for their opinions, so that they are effectively silenced and excluded. Given the trauma involved, their silencing is likely to make matters even worse. It is all the more amazing that, even though they very often suffer long-term damage, so many children cope so heroically (Mullender et al., 2002).

Why does it happen? Explanations

There are many ways of explaining domestic violence in both the sociological and psychological literature, and no single, convincing explanation as to why it happens has been identified. Historically, the overriding attitude to domestic violence was the belief that it is a private affair between a husband and a wife and that nobody should interfere unless it is a constant occurrence, or very evidently causing serious and visible injury. Traditional attitudes, in which the chastisement of wives is seen as a male entitlement that goes along with the territory of marriage, still often hold sway. From this perspective, it is a man's right, or at least his duty, to keep "his" household in order and to ensure that his wife and children do what he says (Dobash & Dobash, 1980). This understanding of domestic abuse is still very important worldwide, although change is occurring to some extent.

In a more academic perspective, individual pathology models are often used in psychology, counselling and psychiatry to explain domestic violence. This kind of explanation is based on the idea that the individual using violence suffers from a pathological condition which leads to deviance from a non-violent norm. In practice, it might only be quite extreme forms of violence or repeated violence that would be included in this kind of diagnosis. A degree of conflict or "low-level" aggression might be seen as "normal", at least in some families. Pathological deviance, however, might be thought to be based on either psychiatric illness or faults of temperament in one or both partners. In this analysis, dysfunctional families are to blame. Domestic violence is not seen as being to do with families in general, but rather with a system of pathology requiring psychiatric or social work intervention.

According to some biological and evolutionary psychological theories, men are biologically aggressive and women biologically passive. One might term such a view "the cows and bulls argument". Of course, there may be some truth in biological arguments, and high doses of testosterone do make both men and women behave more aggressively. However, these days we are expected to be able to control base biological instincts. Men buy their meat from the supermarket, rather than going out and hunting it down.

Sociobiological explanations are a variant of the biological theories, and have much in common with traditional viewpoints, with the superiority of men over women being seen as a biosocial necessity dating from the past, or from genetic imperatives. In this view, there is an evolutionary need for men to be dominant. These explanations often draw upon comparisons with selected non-human species, particularly the primate apes. They propose that modern man is a frustrated version of "Man the Hunter", blocked by modern social organisation and egalitarian ideas of relations between the sexes (Hague & Malos, 2005).

Socio-structural and social constructionist perspectives look at violence in the family in relation to society, and depict violence as being generated by modern society (Straus & Gelles, 1990). Violence in popular culture, for example, is often promoted and even glorified. Movies and men's magazines often feature men being aggressive and using weapons, and women being passive and scantily clad. The boys' section of toyshops can resemble a military arsenal.

In addition, socio-structural explanations may call on "strain theory". In this analysis, social conditions, poor opportunities for life fulfilment, poverty and oppression may lead to strain, frustration and domestic violence. This is an important analysis. It bases itself on the stress caused by lack of access to money, opportunities, housing and education common to both men and women in the family. What it does not really explain is why these tensions lead to men, but not women, becoming violent to their partners or, indeed, why men may be aggressive to their partners, but not to anyone else (Hague & Malos, 2005).

Moralist explanations of domestic violence are often based on ideas about the breakdown of the family caused by a decline in morality and family values. This kind of explanation may hark back to a "golden past", notably the Victorian era, when families were stable and happy and moral deterioration had yet to occur. According to proponents of this thesis, things were better in a previous golden age. However, domestic violence was just as common, or perhaps more common in the past (Dobash & Dobash, 1980).

There are a range of other theories which can be used in thinking about domestic violence, including analyses stressing that some women may be violence-prone or masochistic. These ideas may have some truth in them in rare instances, but it must be said that refuge workers do not come across women who have wanted to be assaulted. A woman may be desperate not to lose a man, or their relationship, but she always wants to be rid of violence.

Some theories stress the intergenerational transmission of violence, in which women and men who witness or experience violence in childhood are more likely to become perpetrators or victims. This certainly does happen, but it is also important to remember that very often it does not. Certainly, then, this is not a universal causal explanation (Hague & Malos, 2005).

Fragmenting Family?

All of these theories contain a kernel of truth. Academic analysts may join bits of them together. However, what is lacking from too many of them is an understanding of the gender dimension of domestic violence. Feminist theorists quite specifically and deliberately bring such understandings into the spotlight. Feminists work in various different schools of thought, including standpoint theory and post-structuralism (for a general introduction to these theories, see Harding, 1987). All of these theories acknowledge that domestic violence is an extraordinarily complex issue, but emphasise the need to incorporate an understanding of power in the family, and of women's position within it. Thus, a feminist understanding might consider a range of factors, but would always be interpreted through a gender-aware lens. This would involve looking at issues of power and control between men and women in intimate relationships, and the connections between having power or greater physical strength, and feeling able to abuse those who do not. Feminist explanations are generally acknowledged by contemporary policymakers and practitioners and tend, in the broader view, to identify violence against women as a manifestation of gender oppression and the still inferior position of women worldwide.

What is being done about it?: Policy responses, services and activism

Domestic violence policy and practice has been transformed beyond recognition in the last thirty years, with hugely improved services in the UK and many other countries (Taylor-Browne, 2001). However, it should be recognised that, whilst long-term campaigning and activism has led to a gradual change in public attitudes, many women and children seeking to escape domestic violence, even in the UK, experience little improvement in their situation. Documents in which survivors are given voice refer again and again to inadequate services, to cutbacks and inaccessible services, and to having to go from one agency to another, and then to another, in order to obtain help (Mullender & Hague, 2001; Humphreys & Thiara, 2002). Nevertheless, improvements have been substantial in relation to policy responses to domestic violence, which have gradually shifted the problem from the margins to the mainstream.

The central plank of all domestic violence policies is women's services. Specialised women-run local domestic violence projects exist in all major towns and cities. In the UK, the refuge movement forms part of the broader international movement against domestic violence. This consists of various loose-knit campaigns, groups, networks and international initiatives (for example, the 1993 UN Declaration on Domestic Violence and the 1995 Beijing Global Platform for Action). Despite high, enduring levels of violence against women worldwide, a global effort is occurring in almost every country of the world, with rapid change happening in many non-Western nations and regions (see, for example, Davies, 1994; see also Garcia-Moreno, Jansen, Ellsberg, Heise & Watts, 2005).

In Britain, the original passion and inspirational impetus displayed by women in the 1970s has led to activism on domestic violence now being far more organised and acknowledged. The activist network includes the four Women's Aid Federations (one in each country of the UK), in conjunction with campaigning groups, including Southall Black Sisters, Justice for Women, Imkaan, the Truth About Rape Campaign, Rights of Women, as well as the End of Violence Against Women Coalition established in late 2005. Women's Aid now runs hundreds of refuges, advocacy, outreach and support services, and also lobbies for national changes in law and policy.

Local domestic violence refuge services include specialist projects for black women and children and for women and children from minority ethnic communities. There is an extensive network of South Asian women's refuges and there are also some specialist refuges for women without children, women who have experienced sexual abuse, and women with learning difficulties or other special needs (Hague & Malos, 2005; http//:www. womensaid.org.uk). In recent years, the growth in the establishment of outreach and advocacy services has led to calls for these to become universally available and to include specific outreach services for black and minority ethnic women and disabled women (Kelly & Humphreys, 2001; Humphreys & Thiara, 2002; Hague, Thiara, Mullender & Magowan, 2008). The overriding aim and ethos of all of these domestic violence services and campaigns is the empowerment of women and children to resist violence against them and to build violence-free lives (Hague & Malos, 2005).

Women's Aid has been instrumental in many of the new policy developments that have transformed services and it now takes a key strategic role with government. This has led to developments in most agencies and government departments. Currently, the Home Office has become the lead government agency, and an important Inter-Departmental Ministerial Group on Domestic Violence has been established, together with an All-Party Parliamentary Group on Violence Against Women. All of this has led to change for the better. The government has made much in the last ten years of saying that it is now committed to a co-ordinated approach to tackling domestic violence and to improving resourcing.

In 2004, the Domestic Violence Crime and Victims Act came into force. The Act strengthened both the criminal law in terms of the prosecution of perpetrators, and the civil law in terms of the enforcement and widening in scope of injunctions against violent men, to stop them molesting their partners. Legislative change has also included the introduction of a new offence of causing or abetting the death of a child or vulnerable adult, and the setting up of domestic homicide reviews. Common assault is to become an arrestable offence. These developments are all helpful. However, despite it being a clear step forward, the Act has proved to be a disappointment in relation to the narrowness of its scope (Kelly & Lovett, 2005). This is because some of the positive and wide-ranging proposals that featured in the previous government consultation paper, *Safety and Justice* (Home Office, 2003), are absent from the new Act, which concentrates solely on criminal and civil justice.

The underlying principle of all work on domestic violence needs to be the safety of the victims. Safety planning with women and children in affected families is a key professional duty. Currently, the aims of policy and practice interventions are often viewed as twofold, to provide support to women and children, and to hold abusers accountable. Three basic areas have been laid down by government in *Safety and Justice* and in the new Act. These are "prevention", "protection" and "support for victims". Together, these form a helpful guide as to how domestic abuse should be dealt with (Home Office, 2003).

The Home Office has now put in place a "National Delivery Action Plan", to progress co-ordinated work on the issue (Home Office, 2008). This has led, very importantly, to the establishment of Specialist Domestic Violence Courts [SDVCs] across the country, and of "Coordinated Community Responses", including Multi-

Agency Risk Assessment Conferences [MARACs] and the employment of Independent Domestic Violence Advisers [IDVAs] to offer support (usually in high risk cases) (Home Office, 2007/8). These developments have also been accompanied by a modest funding commitment to improve refuge provision, alongside partial funding for the national helpline. "Supporting People" finance is available for women in refuge accommodation and to provide floating support. Thanks to these initiatives, domestic violence is now beginning to creep up the crime prevention and other strategic agendas.

Nonetheless, an integrated national strategy on violence against women is still lacking, although the government is currently conducting consultations on developing one. Certainly, then, there have been improvements. The new legislation presented a golden opportunity for the UK to develop a co-ordinated and comprehensive approach to domestic violence. However, the golden opportunity has not quite made it through into practice, but the possibility is now there.

Working to a range of Home Office circulars, the police response to domestic violence has improved markedly. This has been achieved through the adoption of what is termed "positive policing", pro-prosecution policies and the provision of support for women and child victims through police domestic violence units and domestic violence liaison officers (Home Office, 1990; 2000). Perpetrator programmes have been set up (although often operating on a small scale) and there are attempts to take the onus away from the victim by proposed changes in relation to the central importance attached to her providing evidence in court.

Domestic violence policies exist to improve responses in most statutory agencies. For example, the Crown Prosecution has developed excellent good practice policies

(Crown Prosecution Service, 2008). The health and social services have also developed good practice guidelines, policies and service responses (Department of Health, 2005; Hague & Malos, 2005). The government has encouraged the setting up of multi-agency and inter-agency forums, bringing together all of the relevant statutory and voluntary sector agencies in a local area in order to build co-ordinated local responses. More than 200 of these exist up and down the country, developing policy, setting up new services, and attempting to integrate services without becoming "talking shops" (Hague, Malos & Dear, 1996). Importantly, domestic violence is now the subject of wider partnership and strategy work across localities, as it has gradually become mainstreamed into the local "strategic agenda".

Access to temporary, emergency and permanent housing has been improved through homelessness legislation, including the Housing (Homeless Persons) Act 1977, the Housing Act 1996, and the Homelessness Act 2002. These are all essential resources for women and children who are homeless because of domestic violence. On the other hand, permanent social housing stocks are gradually disappearing in this country, with properties being bought up and leaving the public domain. In some localities, women and children accepted for rehousing have to wait for very long periods in revolving cycles of temporary accommodation (Levison & Harwin, 2001, p. 167).

Social services have begun to take domestic violence seriously as a child protection issue after years of neglect and ignoring of the issue (Farmer & Owen, 1995). Many social services departments now have domestic violence policies, employ specialists in domestic violence posts, liaise closely with the police, and attempt to pay attention to domestic abuse for disabled and older women as well as to cases involving vulnerable children. Children's charities have also taken up the issue of domestic violence to a greater or lesser extent, especially in relation to child protection (e.g. the NSPCC and Barnardo's). Overall, new services are more and more frequently accompanied by training for professionals on domestic violence.

However, the picture is not as rosy in reality as it might appear in theory. Resources are still massively lacking in this area of work, and the problems of uneven or fragmented services and a lack of systematic comprehensive funding continue to characterise approaches to domestic violence in the UK. Currently, owing to the development of generic services, many local domestic violence services are under threat, especially those serving black and minority ethnic communities (Gill, 2008).

The movement again -- and the future

After a historical lack of regard for the issue which stretches back through time, we are currently living through a period of unprecedented interest in domestic violence and its impact on families. This is largely due to activism on the issue. Rebecca and Russell Dobash said back in 1992: "The great mobilisation of women began by a vision supported by action. Their vision was of a world transformed" (Dobash & Dobash, 1992, p. 9). Both then and now, activists against domestic violence have brought women together, both those who have experienced violence and those who have not, in an often inspiring way. Transformation and empowerment remain as the central concepts to women's activism on domestic violence, together with ideas about self-determination for women and collective action (Schechter, 1982; Dobash & Dobash, 1992; Hague & Malos, 2005). Working as part of a vibrant social movement for women, activists make connections across diversity, whilst recognising the challenges and difficulties posed by cultural difference. Domestic violence is now acknowledged as a massive problem worldwide, and there is change in the air globally.

Of course, the slowness of such change can be frustrating. Resources are always overstretched and women's organisations and campaigns against gender violence can sometimes appear to be struggling hopelessly against overwhelming odds. That said, enormous achievements have been made both nationally and globally. It is important to acknowledge the debt owed to the movements against domestic violence, to celebrate the enormous changes and to recognise the new history that we are all making. Anyone who was politically aware before the seventies will be able to confirm how much things have been transformed in the UK and elsewhere.

There is inspiration and solace to be found in women's resistance to male violence and abuse in the family. We need to hold on to this celebration, academically, professionally and personally, despite the fact that the reality of trying to put a stop to the abuse of women and children in families can seem overwhelming at times. However, we now walk on new historical ground, as domestic violence is beginning to be taken seriously at last.

In the making of this new history, professionally and personally, it is important to preserve and to be guided by the enduring and passionate vision of domestic violence activists, of a world in which women can live abuse-free lives, where families can be safe for women, and where male violence against women is finally a thing of the past.

References

Amos, V., & Parmar, P. (1984). Challenging imperial feminism. *Feminist Review*, 17, 3-19.

Barrett, M., & McIntosh, M. (1982). *The anti-social family*. London: NLB.

Crown Prosecution Service. (2008). *CPS: Guidance on prosecuting cases of domestic violence* (Rev. ed). Retrieved July 14, 2009, from: http://www. cps.gov.uk/publications/prosecution/domestic/dov_ guidance.html

Davies, M. (1994). *Women and violence: Realities and responses world-wide*. London: Zed Books.

Demo, D. H., Allen, K. R., & Fine, M. A. (Eds.). (2000) *Handbook of family diversity.* New York: Oxford University Press.

Department of Health. (2005). *Responses to domestic abuse: A handbook for health professionals*. London: Department of Health.

Dobash, R. E., & Dobash, R. P. (1980). *Violence against wives*. London: Open Books.

Dobash, R. E., & Dobash, R. P. (1992). *Women, violence, and social change.* London: Routledge.

Domestic Violence, Crime and Victims Act: Elizabeth II, 2004, Chapter 28 (2004). London: Stationery Office.

Donovan, C., & Hester, M. (2008). 'Because she was my first girlfriend, I didn't know any different': making the case for mainstreaming same-sex sex/relationship education. *Sex Education, (8)* 3, 277-288.

Farmer, E., & Owen, M. (1995). *Decision-making, intervention and outcome in child protection work.* London: Department of Health.

Garcia-Moreno, C., Jansen, H. A. F. M., Ellsberg, M., Heise, L., & Watts, C. (2005). *WHO multi-country study on health and domestic violence against women: Initial results on prevalence, health outcomes and women's responses.* Geneva: World Health Organization.

Gill, A., & Banga, B. (2008). A specialist refuge space of my own: BMER women, housing and domestic violence. *Ethnicity and Inequalities in Health and Social Care, 1* (2), 24-34.

Hague, G., & Malos, E. (2005). *Domestic violence: Action for change* (3rd ed.). Cheltenham: New Clarion Press. (Original ed. published 1993).

Hague, G., Malos, E. and Dear, W. (1996). *Multi-agency work and domestic violence.* Bristol: Policy Press.

Hague, G., Thiara, R., Mullender, A., & Magowan, P. (2008). *Making the links: Disabled women and domestic violence. Good practice guidance.* Bristol: Women's Aid.

Hague, G. , & Wilson, C. (1996). *The Silenced Pain.* Bristol: Policy Press.

Harding, S. (1987). *Feminism and methodology.* Buckingham: Open University Press.

Hester, M., Pearson, C. & Harwin, N., with Abrahams, H. (2007). *Making an impact: Children and domestic violence* (2nd ed.). London: Jessica Kingsley Publishers.

Home Office. (1990). *Domestic violence: Circular 60/90.* London: Home Office.

Home Office. (2000). *Domestic violence: Circular 19/2000.* (Rev. ed.). London: Home Office.

Home Office. (2003). *Safety and justice: The government's proposals on domestic violence.* London: Home Office.

Home Office. (2005). *Domestic violence: A national report.* Retrieved July 14, 2009, from: http://www.crimereduction.homeoffice. gov.uk/ domesticviolence/domesticviolence.pdf

Home Office. (2008). *National Domestic Violence Delivery Plan: Annual progress report, 2007-08.* London: Home Office.

Housing Act: Elizabeth II, 1996, Chapter 52 (1996). London: Stationery Office.

Housing (Homeless Persons) Act: Elizabeth II, 1977, Chapter 48 (1977). London: HMSO.

Homelessness Act: Elizabeth II, 2002, Chapter 7 (2002). London: Stationery Office.

Humphreys, C., & Thiara, R. (2002). *Routes to safety: Protection issues facing abused women and children and the role of outreach services.* Bristol: Women's Aid Federation of England.

Kelly, L. (1988). *Surviving sexual violence.* Cambridge: Polity Press.

Kelly, L. (1994). The inter-connectedness of domestic violence and child abuse. In A. Mullender & R. Morley (Eds.), *Children living with domestic violence Putting men's abuse of women on the child care agenda* (pp. 43-56). London: Whiting & Birch.

Kelly, L., & Humphreys, C. (2001). Supporting women and children in their communities: Outreach and advocacy approaches to domestic violence. In J. Taylor-Browne (Ed.), *What works in reducing domestic violence: A comprehensive guide for professionals* (pp. 239-73). London: Whiting & Birch.

Kelly, L., & Lovett, J. (2005). *What a waste: The case for an integrated violence against women strategy.* London: Department of Trade and Industry.

Lasch, C. (1995). *Haven in a heartless world: The family besieged* (New ed.). New York: Norton. (Original ed. published 1977).

Levison, D., & Harwin, N. (2001). Accommodation provision. In J. Taylor-Browne (Ed.), *What works in reducing domestic violence: A comprehensive guide for professionals* (pp. 151-186). London: Whiting & Birch.

Mullender, A. (2004). *Tackling domestic violence: Providing support for children who have witnessed domestic violence.*

London: Home Office, Research, Development and Statistics Directorate.

Mullender, A., & Hague, G. (2001). Women survivors' views. In J. Taylor-Browne (Ed.), *What works in reducing domestic violence: A comprehensive guide for professionals* (pp. 1-34). London: Whiting & Birch.

Mullender, A., Hague, G., Imam, U. F., Kelly, L., Malos, E., & Regan, L. (2002). *Children's perspectives on domestic violence.* London: Sage Publications.

Mullender, A., & Morley, R. (Eds.). (1994). *Children living with domestic violence: Putting men's abuse of women on the child care agenda.* London: Whiting & Birch.

Muncie, J., Cochrane, A., Dallos, R., & Wetherell, M. (Eds.). (1995). *Understanding the family: Public definitions and private lives* (Rev. ed.). London: Sage Publications.

Schechter, S. (1982). *Women and male violence: The visions and struggles of the Battered Women's Movement.* London: Pluto Press.

Stanko, E. A., Crisp, D., Hale, C., & Lucraft, H. (1998). *Counting the costs: Estimating the impact of domestic violence in the London Borough of Hackney.* London: Crime Concern.

Stark, E. (2007). *Coercive control: How men entrap women in personal life.* Oxford: Oxford University Press.

Straus, M. A., & Gelles, R. J. (1990). *Physical violence in American families: risk factors and adaptations to violence in 8,145 families.* New Brunswick, NJ: Transaction Publishers.

Taylor-Browne, J. (Ed.). (2001). *What works in reducing domestic violence: A comprehensive guide for professionals.* London: Whiting & Birch.

UNICEF. (1997). *The progress of nations, 1997: [The nations of the world ranked according to their achievements in child health, nutrition, education, family planning and progress for women].* New York: Author.

Walby, S., & Allen, J. (2004). *Domestic violence, sexual assault and stalking: Findings from the British Crime Survey.* London: Home Office.

Walker, L. (1984). *The battered woman syndrome.* New York: Springer.

THE GENDERED NATURE OF WORK-LIFE BALANCE[1]

Louise Wattis, Kay Standing, Susanna Lloyd and Julie Lewis

Introduction

In recent years, work-life balance has emerged as a definite concern and a focus for social policy within Western post-industrial societies. This is in part because of changing patterns of paid employment brought about by the globalised 24/7 economy, the growth of the service sector, and the decline in secure "traditional" employment. Such changes have rendered paid work an increasingly demanding and stressful experience (Taylor, 2000). Employment in countries such as the USA and the UK is now characterised by exceptionally long working hours (Hochschild, 1997; Eurostat, 2002; Office for National Statistics, 2003). Post-Fordist working conditions mean that maintaining sufficient boundaries between work, leisure and home life is increasingly difficult. Taylor argues that such changes have resulted in increasing pressure on the individual with regards to their relationship to work. He argues that this goes beyond the issues of balancing work and parenting which "remains much too narrow an approach for our understanding of the importance of the work-life debate" (Taylor, 2000, p. 7). Women's increased entry into paid employment and the rise in dual-earner households means that divisions between unpaid and paid work are no longer straightforward. This has resulted in a "crisis of care" (Fraser, 1994), which renders negotiating

---

[1] This chapter reports on research undertaken by the four authors. It was delivered as a paper at Chester by Louise Wattis.

73

these boundaries especially problematic for those with caring responsibilities (Glass & Estes, 1997; Duncan, 2002). This is further exacerbated by uncompromising organisational structures and, in the UK context, by a lack of affordable and available childcare (Daycare Trust, 2001) and the prevalence of the long hours work culture (Eurostat, 2002; Kodz et al., 2003; Flexecutive, 2004).

This issue is also highly gendered. Care continues to lack social and economic value (Land, 1980) and is mainly viewed as a feminine occupation (Voet, 1998). Although women now participate in paid work, there is still an expectation that they will take primary responsibility for childcare and domestic arrangements. Part-time work remains the principal means of managing both. However, women's part-time employment choices have significant implications for employment progression and labour market position (Rubery, Horrell & Burchell, 1994; Rubery & Fagan, 1995).

In recognition of the pressures faced by working parents, and with the aim of promoting greater female labour market participation, the UK government has introduced a number of policy measures aimed at childcare provision. These include flexible working, leave arrangements, and providing financial incentives for working parents. However, the adequacy of UK "family-friendly" policy is questionable (Moss, 2001; McKie, Gregory & Bowlby, 2002). Parental leave and flexible working legislation is weak in comparison with other European countries (Moss, 2001; Hantrais, 2004), and employees' access to family-friendly flexible working arrangements is inconsistent and limited within certain employment sectors. Moreover, it is clear that UK policy prioritises the market and employers (Auer, 2002). Duncan (2002) argues that the UK is caught between EU policy, which advocates legislation in the interests of the employee, and the deregulated and less "employee-friendly" US labour market. Policy also appears to be aimed at women, which perpetuates the feminisation of the caring role and women's social and economic inequality (Lister, 1998).

This paper will explore the gendered nature of the work-care issue and the effectiveness and availability of family-friendly policy in the UK, highlighting the highly gendered conditions in which individuals undertake work and care decisions. It is acknowledged that this issue encompasses a much wider range of responsibilities than parenting, such as the care of elderly and disabled relatives. However, this paper will focus on childcare, given its impact on women's employment patterns.

Family-friendly policy in the UK

UK government policy since the late 1990s has aimed at reducing the pressures of combining work and family, and encouraging participation in paid work via a number of policy measures and benefit reforms. This is evident in the 1998 National Childcare Strategy, which pledged to address the shortage of formal childcare provision. It proposed to do this by partially subsidising childcare costs for parents through the provision of a variety of childcare services for children of all ages, delivered by childcare partnerships and led by local authorities. This has resulted in the creation of one million part-time nursery education places for all three- and four-year olds. This initiative also led to the setting up of Sure Start programmes, which aim to provide health and educational support for 0-4 year olds in deprived areas. The current government ultimately aims to establish a children's centre in every community across the country, at which parents and children can access health and childcare services and parental support. More recently, the government's 10-year childcare strategy pledged to provide wrap-around primary school-based childcare from 8am till 6pm, and proposed to widen availability for 11-14 year olds by the end of a third term of office (Blair, 2004).

In 2000, the government set up a Ministerial Review and the Work and Parents Taskforce to consult with businesses, academics, trade unions and groups representing parents and employees, to ascertain how best to implement and promote work-life balance policy. Central issues identified within the Green Paper (Department of Trade and Industry [DTI], 2000) were the need to support working parents, while also supporting businesses in adopting family-friendly, flexible working practices. The Green Paper was part of a raft of consultation, legislation and campaigning around the issue of employment flexibility and work-life balance. Following the consultation process, the government introduced a range of employee and parent "friendly" legislative measures and amendments to tax and benefit systems. This also led to the revising of existing policy and the launching of the DTI Work Life Balance Campaign in 2000. Further rights for working parents had been evident in the 1999 Employment Relations Act. It introduced the EU Parental Leave Directive (Council of the European Union, 1996), which granted parents the right to unpaid leave to look after children under six, and also provided for time off for dependants. In addition, following a further review of parental rights in 2001, the 2002 Employment Bill enhanced maternity leave entitlements by introducing paid paternity leave and leave for adoptive parents. The 2002 Employment Act also granted parents with children under six or disabled children under the age of 18 the right to request flexible work arrangements. Further amendments to tax and benefit systems were introduced in 2003 and represent "the latest stage in the process of reform" (Pion Economics, 2003, p. 13). The main aim is to make the system more straightforward for working parents, particularly those on low incomes. From April 2003 entitlement to tax credit is based on annual income. Child Tax Credit and Working Tax Credit now replace previous tax credits and benefits and operate under a single system, which corresponds to the tax system as a whole.

More recently, the Work and Families Act (2006) has placed flexible working firmly on the UK policy agenda and has improved maternity and adoption rights and pay in the UK; maternity leave is now the longest in Europe and maternity pay has doubled. The Work and Family Act also introduced additional paternity leave and, crucially, extended the flexible working request to carers of adults. The UK has thus moved towards a more supportive rhetoric, with demands for the government to extend flexible working rights to all. However, research indicates that supportive rhetoric at policy and employer level often fails to translate into the reality of working practices (Parent-Thirion, Fernández Macías, Hurley & Vermeylen, 2007).

New Labour policy has stressed the importance of paid work for the social and personal well-being of the individual and for the good of society more broadly. This is evident within citizenship discourses and debates on the "third way" (Lister, 2000; McKie, Bowlby & Gregory, 2001; Rake, 2001). Policy aims to address the welfare dependency of lone parents (Lewis, Mitchell, Woodland, Fell, & Gloyer, 2001; Evans, Eyre, Millar & Sarre, 2003) through the tax credit system, where the aim is to "make work pay" (Department of Social Security [DSS], 1998). New Deal schemes targeting young people, lone parents, the long-term unemployed and partners of the long-term unemployed were also introduced in the late 1990s to provide guidance to enable these groups to re-enter the labour market. As Dean (2002) observes, "the principal thrust of New Labour's policy is to promote the idea that all parents should be able to combine paid work and family life" (p. 6). Much of the emphasis is upon retaining mothers within the labour force through enhanced maternity rights, variable working options, and improved childcare provision. Nonetheless, it is clear that the priority is greater productivity and improved economic performance, rather than gender equity (Squires & Wickham-Jones, 2004). As Lister (2000) argues, gender equality has not been a key concern for New Labour, which views feminism as "yesterday's politics" (Coote, 2001, p. 3; as cited in Lister, 2000).

Problems with family-friendly policy

UK work-life family-friendly policy is problematic on a number of levels. Despite government rhetoric promoting work-life balance and flexible working as a "win-win" situation for both working parents and employers, there is a clear divergence between the interests of employers and employees. Prior to the introduction of legislation in 2003, representatives from employers' organisations expressed reservations regarding the prospect of enforcing mandatory measures, particularly concerning the automatic right for employees to work part-time (Hall, 2001). The views of business clearly influenced the government's decision to impose "light-touch", voluntary legislation that ultimately gives employers the final say as to whether employees may be granted the right to work flexibly. The effectiveness of this is questionable, especially when one considers the fact that mandatory measures continue to be abused. For instance, pregnant women continue to suffer discrimination and dismissal (Equal

Opportunities Commission [EOC], 2004b), and employers continue to flout the EU Working Time Directive, which aims to reduce average working hours to a 48-hour weekly maximum (Hogarth et al., 2003; EOC, 2004a). It has been observed that UK legislation demonstrates "areas of vagueness and inconsistency" and as a result will have no real impact on employees' working experiences, but may result in a flood of employment disputes and tribunals because of ambiguities and the absence of any "clear framework" (Flexibility.co.uk); furthermore, that family-friendly legislation demonstrates no real recognition of the diverse and changing needs of working parents (Hogarth, Hasluck, Pierre, Winterbotham, & Vivian, 2000; McKie et al., 2001, 2002).

Evidence suggests that flexible working practices and "family-friendly" policy may only become acceptable in certain sectors and organisations, and at certain levels (Dex & Scheibl, 2002; Fagan, 2005) and may be viewed as incompatible with senior level and managerial occupation (Flexecutive, 2004). The fact that so many employers flout working time regulations is indicative of the persistence of traditional workplace cultures and long hours of work, which oppose forms of working that are compatible with the dual responsibilities of home and family (EOC, 2000; Hogarth et al., 2000; Rake, 2001). There is a danger of flexible working becoming concentrated in public sector organisations and large private sector firms that wish to retain experienced and highly skilled employees (Glass & Estes, 1997; Fagan, 2005). On the other hand, firms may offer flexible working opportunities to lower level employees, whilst higher level management positions demand long and inflexible hours (Crompton, 2002). In addition, it is likely that organisations "window dress" or overstate their work-life balance policies. Often, access to flexibility is far removed from what is expressed in company policy (Hogarth et al., 2000; Dex & Scheibl, 2002) and employees are reluctant to use such policies due to hostile workplace cultures (Kodz, Harper & Dench, 2002).

In relation to childcare provision, Rake (2001) argues that the National Childcare Strategy fails to deliver consistent services across the country because of its implementation at the local level. Moreover, free state nursery places offer little opportunity to combine paid and caring work, as daily sessions only last for two and half hours. Consequently, gaps in provision mean that "the constraints of childcare will remain a strong influence on the labour market decisions of parents, particularly mothers of young children" (Rake, p. 223). Rake notes that no attempt is made to encourage men's participation in caring and domestic roles. The fact that parental leave is unpaid is evidence of this, as is the opt-out of the EU Working Time Directive, which could have addressed the UK long-hours culture and potentially enabled men to take on a more active caring role.

There are fundamental problems with both government and organisational policies. This relates to specific features of legislation, and also the way in which policy is interpreted and operationalised within the workplace. There is evidence to suggest that adopting flexible working practices can be beneficial to employers (Dex & Smith, 2002). However, organisational cultures that promote long hours and inflexible employer-led working arrangements mean that it is difficult for employee-led flexibility to be accepted as normalised employment practice (Kodz et al., 2002). As Crompton and Birkelund (2000) note, there is an inescapable tension between "family-friendly" policy and the demands of the market. This transcends national boundaries and is felt most intensely within professional occupations such as banking, in which full-time, inflexible commitment is required in order to progress. Crompton and Birkelund go on to claim that this is exacerbated by trends promoting individualised performance and competition, rendering higher level occupations within certain sectors as "those least compatible with employment and caring" (2000, p. 349). Thus, at a time when family-friendly employment is being touted as essential to enable the reconciliation of work and care, market trends appear to be going in the opposite direction. Moreover, at the lower end of the labour market, there is little to suggest that government policy favours the interests of low-income families over those of business (Dean, 2002).

Even if the practical elements relating to the availability and awareness of work-life balance legislation were unproblematic, matters of work and care represent a much more complex issue, one that the legislation and UK family policy in general fails to recognise. Such policy inadequacies run far deeper than the practicalities of access and availability and need to be analysed in much wider terms in order to acknowledge the significance of gender. The next section will set this issue in the context of EU policy, before considering the gendered implications of the work and care issue.

Family-friendly policy in Europe

UK "family-friendly" policy since 1997 has largely been prompted by a series of EU directives aimed at addressing leave entitlements, part-time rights and working hours. The welfare of working parents has been identified as an explicit objective of EU employment guidelines and the EU Social Policy Agenda. These seek to "reconcile employment and care responsibilities in light of the demise of the "male breadwinner" model of employment and the ascendancy of both dual-earner and single parent families"

(Fagan, 2005, p. 23). The European Commission has also outlined its commitment to gender equality via its "gender mainstreaming" initiative, described in a European Commission Communication in 2000 as "integrating the gender equality objective into the policies that have a direct or indirect impact on the lives of women and men". However, commitment to gender equity and the welfare of working parents is also precarious, given that the EU was formed initially to secure the economic interests of member states (Guerrina, 2002).

EU-led policy in this area includes the Working Time, Parental Leave and Part-Time Working Directives. The EU adopted the Part-Time Workers Directive in June 1997. In the UK, the Part-Time Workers (Prevention of Less Favourable Treatment) Regulations were implemented on July 1, 2000 (Statutory Instruments, 2000), and were amended in 2002. In general, this legislation aims to ensure that part-time employees are treated no less favourably than equivalent employees in terms of pro rata pay, company pensions, and access to training and holiday and leave entitlements (Nickson, 2004). In 1995, the EU set out a framework for parental leave, its aim being "the reconciliation of work and family life", proposing the "better organisation of working hours and greater flexibility, and for an easier return to working life" (Council of the European Union, 1996, p. 1). Entitlement to leave was introduced in the EU in June 1998, and in the UK as part of the 1999 Employment Act. The Working Time Directive (93/104EC) was introduced in the UK in 1998 and stipulated a statutory limit of a 48-hour working week, as well as legal entitlements to paid leave and rest breaks. However, despite the working time regulations, the long-hours culture persists and employers continue to flout rules regarding working hours (Flexecutive, 2004). The UK is the only member state that permits staff to "opt out" of the 48-hour maximum limit on working hours. Guerrina (2002) claims that EU family-friendly policy demonstrates no real commitment to equality and concern for women's social and economic welfare, and has mainly been provoked by a concern with declining fertility rates, ageing populations, and the need to maximise labour force participation "to ensure the stability of population numbers and the future viability of the welfare state" (Guerrina, p. 52). Guerrina further argues that EU policy lays a framework for legal equality for women, but provides only minimum protection for working mothers and fails to address the structures that perpetuate social inequality and conflicts between work and care.

> The direction of EU policies at the end of the last decade has been to allow men and women to reconcile employment in the official labour market and family life. However, despite this shift, the failure of member states' governments to challenge structural inequalities continues to separate rhetoric from reality and reaffirms traditional divisions of labour. (Guerrina, 2002, p. 63)

Such limitations are evident in UK legislation, in which care provisions and family-friendly policies are some of the weakest in Europe (Moss, 2001). The UK advocates a gendered division of care and paid work (Pfau-Effinger, 1999), which promotes women's employment, but also their role as main carers. This results in an adapted "breadwinner model", in which women will often work part-time. State provision for childcare is patchy in the UK. When women work full-time, childcare is generally provided by the private sector or informally. Since 1997, the UK has moved towards a more supportive discourse. However, as Hantrais observes, "family policy has not become a legitimate and fully institutionalised policy domain" (2004, p. 161). For example, statutory leave is the weakest in Europe, there is no entitlement to publicly funded early years education, and no statutory right to reduced working hours (Moss, 2001). This is in contrast to France and the Nordic countries, whose family and care policies are highly legitimated and formalised, with a high standard of flexible services and childcare provision. UK family policy can also be contrasted to Dutch work-care policy, which lacks adequate formal care structures, but advocates work-family reconciliation via employees' rights to reduced working hours (Organisation for Economic Co-operation and Development [OECD], 2002). The Dutch "combination model" recommends part-time work for both parents in order for them to "share the responsibility for unpaid work at home" (Plantenga, 2002, p. 64). However, it is still generally women who work part-time, and so care and work roles in the Netherlands are more likely to resemble the UK male breadwinner model and female part-time carer model (Bang, Jensen, & Pfau-Effinger, 2000). And, even in countries with more structured family policy and enhanced employee rights, occupational segregation and gendered labour markets are still apparent. For example, Sweden provides highly structured state care provision, as well as recognising the place of care within the family. However, as Lewis observes, it demonstrates a highly segregated labour market, with women working predominantly within the public sector, where "the work culture acknowledges the right to time to care" (2001, p. 164). As with other less "family-friendly" states, men in Sweden are more likely to work within the private sector, where care needs are less recognised and long-hours work cultures are more prevalent, again highlighting the significance of working time arrangements. Indeed, even with effective formal provision, if the issue of working hours and work time is not addressed, care will never be redistributed and occupational segregation and labour market inequalities will continue.

Labour market inequality and care and work preferences

Despite increased participation and some labour market gains, women's labour market inequality persists. Statistics for 2002 show that women earned 19% less than men, with figures for average weekly and household income indicating a gap of 25% (EOC, 2001). Vertical segregation highlights women's under-representation at managerial level and above within both public and private sector organisations (Court, 1995). Women are concentrated within a more limited number of occupations and sectors than men. For instance, 60% of the female workforce in the UK is clustered in just ten occupational groups (Walby & Olsen, 2002) within two industrial sectors: public administration, education and health, and distribution, hotels and catering. Jobs in these sectors are more likely to be low skilled and low paid (EOC, 2001), and inequalities are perpetuated via interrelated factors such as organisational structures and cultures, ideologies relating to appropriate gender roles, and the lack of adequate childcare provision (Court, 1995). However, variations between countries exist owing to cultural factors, and also differing welfare regimes and family policies (Hantrais, 2004; Pfau-Effinger, 1999).

Childcare responsibilities and inadequate childcare provision are often cited as key factors contributing to women's fragmented labour force participation and provide a significant barrier to occupational mobility (Dex, 1987; McRae, 1991). Despite the fact that women are now active participants within the labour market, they continue to carry out the bulk of childcare and domestic tasks (Gershuny, Godwin & Jones, 1994; Mansfield & Collard,

1988; Warde & Hetherington, 1993). The principal means by which many women manage dual responsibilities and make up for the lack of available childcare is to work part-time (Fagan, O'Reilly, & Rubery, 1999; Bang et al., 2000; Lewis, 2001). However, part-time work is often clustered within low-status, low paid, service sector occupations that offer little opportunity for training and progression and contribute significantly to women's labour market inequality (Rubery & Fagan, 1995; Rubery, Smith, & Fagan. 1998; Warren, 2000; Jenkins, 2004).

Attitudes towards unpaid care, and who does it, are central when considering labour market inequalities. For instance, Ball notes that "how mothers *feel about* caring for children has been given insufficient attention in current childcare and gender equality policies" (2004, p. 19). Others have observed that care must become a more valued activity in both social and economic terms (Fraser, 1994; Crompton, Gallie & Purcell, 1996; Land, 1999; Lewis, 2001; Williams, 2001; Hantrais, 2004). This is firstly in recognition that caring is an activity which women have historically done, continue to do, and continue to want to do (Duncan, Edwards, Reynolds, & Alldred, 2003); secondly, that if care were recognised and rewarded, men would be more likely to become involved in it (McKie et al., 2001; Fraser, 1994). Moreover, it has been argued that care should become a central focus in analyses of welfare regimes, labour market patterns, demographic shifts and changes in "care relationships" between the state, the family and the market (Daly & Lewis, 2000; Williams, 2001). Such arguments highlight the value of care and make it more visible, drawing attention to how other commitments such as paid work can be effectively reconciled with care commitments, rather than how care can be accommodated around paid work.

The Gendered Nature of Work-Life Balance

Crompton and Harris (1998) have noted the pervasive influence of the "male breadwinner" model, ideologically and materially, upon all aspects of lived experience where it "provided the framework for the construction of major institutions; including welfare regimes, education systems, social security systems, etc. It has also shaped ideas of masculinity and femininity, and of the 'proper' kinds of work for men and women" (p. 131). Lewis (2001) notes that the "adult worker model", in which both men and women are individualised and fully integrated into the labour market, actually represents the new "ought to be" rather than the new "is" in terms of participation within paid work. This has led Crompton (2002) to argue that there has been no fundamental change in the gendered division of labour and no real decline of the "male breadwinner" model. Women may now work, but they do so in a way that enables them to combine this with care and domestic work. As Lewis (2001) further argues, although women are expected to participate in paid work, *how* women work and *which* women work "remains unclear" (p. 158). Women's labour force participation is expected. However, structural and cultural factors do not enable their employment to progress (Duncan, 2002; Guerrina, 2002), and New Labour discourses about citizenship and work (Williams, 2001; Lister, 2003) conflict with still prevalent gender assumptions that continue to frame mothers and women as primarily responsible for care (Voet, 1998). Rake (2001) identifies the implicit presence of gender bias within a raft of post-1997 social policy reform. This is largely owing to the way in which notions of citizenship under New Labour promote mutual obligations and responsibilities between the state and worker that are defined "predominantly through engagement in the labour market" (p. 211). This contributes to "the longstanding undervaluation of unpaid caring work" (p. 226), in tandem with a distinct lack of encouragement for men to "do caring". For instance, Rake argues that, in the drive to encourage lone parents (who are most often lone mothers) into employment, the value of unpaid caring work performed by those on benefit is ignored. In addition, she also highlights the way in which other elements of welfare-to-work schemes and WFTC [Working Families Tax Credit], now Child Tax Credit, actually discourage certain groups of women from paid work, because they are based on joint earnings.

Duncan et al. (2003) claim that the replacement of the "male breadwinner model" with the "adult worker model" has resulted in misconceptions and inaccurate policy assumptions, in which it is assumed that the main preference is towards paid work. The persistence of the "male breadwinner model" in the shaping of work and caring experiences is misunderstood within policy. The reality that many men feel they should care, and more significantly "often wish to do so", is overlooked. Hakim's preference theory (1996; 2000) frames women's orientations to full-time or part-time employment as a matter of voluntary choice, where women working part-time are viewed as lacking commitment to paid work. This approach views work and care preferences as unproblematic. However, Hakim fails to appreciate the poor pay and conditions of much part-time employment (Rubery et al., 1998; Warren, 2000), the impact on pension contributions (Ginn, Street & Arber, 2001), and the implications for women if partnered relationships break down (Rake, 2001; Himmelweit & Sigala, 2002). Most notably, preference theory does not recognise how organisational structures fail to accommodate those with caring responsibilities and how gender ideologies continue to influence women's choices (Crompton & Harris, 1997; 1998).

The Gendered Nature of Work-Life Balance

McKie et al. (2001) observe that the prevalence of ideologies that frame women within the caring role and encourage the continuation of the "conventional" gender "template" are central in shaping labour market experiences and employment trajectories. This is evident in relation to UK family-friendly policies. On the face of it, the aim is to enable *parents* to reconcile work and care. However, it is evident that the primary concern is to retain women's economic activity whilst they continue to take primary responsibility for care. This results in a situation in which women do participate within the labour market, but within the confines of gendered expectations. For instance, unpaid parental leave merely reinforces gendered caring roles, because women are more likely to take the leave as they earn less than men. Leave must be paid leave if men are to be encouraged to "do more caring" and care and work roles are to be reformulated. Bond & Sales (2001), argue that, as long as the present situation persists, women will continue to hold an unequal position within the labour market. They note that this represents something of a vicious circle, as women's "disadvantaged position in employment leads to a continuation of these domestic responsibilities" (p. 245). Lister (2000) also makes this point, identifying childcare as a central barrier to women's active and equal citizenship, which results in the under-representation of women within public life.

Discussion

UK family policy since 1997 should be viewed positively as it successfully demonstrates a recognition of the needs of working parents. Prior to 1997, market deregulation and the then Conservative government's framing of childcare and family as a private responsibility meant that there was little public support for working families within the UK

(Auer, 2002; Hantrais, 2004). In contrast, the introduction of leave entitlements, tax credits, childcare provision frameworks and legislation, albeit "light-touch", represents a much stronger recognition of the need to support working families. For instance, Lister (2003) comments that, despite its flaws, the National Childcare Strategy represents something of a shift away from a liberal philosophy that separates public from private and is "the first time that government has accepted that childcare is a public as well as a private responsibility" (Lister, 2003, p. 432). There is also evidence that flexible working practices are becoming more accepted within organisations, as it becomes increasingly recognised that these practices can be beneficial to employers through enhanced employee performance (Dex & Scheibl, 2002). Himmelweit and Sigala (2003) argue that mothers' care and work decisions can be influenced by policy interventions such as childcare subsidies and tax credits. This suggests that, although this type of measure does not undermine conventional gender assumptions, it does remove some of the barriers to employment and may render labour market participation less problematic for women. However, policy appears weak and based largely on rhetoric, when compared to the highly structured and established care provision and leave entitlements offered in France and the Nordic countries. Moreover, the flexible working request is clear evidence that government prioritises the needs of employers over employees. As Moss (2001, p. 11) comments: "Government is trying to ride two horses: supporting families and minimising regulation". This is also made evident by the continuing prevalence of a long-hours working culture in the UK and the failure of legislation to address this problem effectively.

A lack of understanding of the way that policies impact upon gendered experiences of work and care is clearly evident within several aspects of government policy. First, the potential for the tax credit system to discourage women's participation in paid work (Lewis, 2001). Secondly, the failure to address the long-hours working culture or introduce paid parental leave does little to promote men's participation in caring activities and helps to reinforce the traditional gendered work/care roles. There is the possibility that flexible working and leave policies may become a means by which women manage dual roles, just as they do in relation to part-time work. By such means, these concerns become "women's issues" (Guerrina, 2002) and policy acts to maintain established "gender contracts" rather than encouraging a re-evaluation of the status of care and its redistribution.

> Reconciling paid work and family life means more than increasing women's access to paid work (the equal opportunities at work agenda); it instead implies a redistribution of work and status between women and men that is changing the gender contract. (Duncan, 2002, p. 307)

In practical terms, UK family-friendly policy demonstrates significant inadequacies and does little to address the gender imbalances apparent between paid work and care work. However, it has also been shown that even where practical reconciliation is more effective, as is the case in Scandinavia, similar work/care roles exist (Crompton & Birkelund, 2000; Lewis, 2001). This highlights the persistence of conventional assumptions about gender roles. Guerrina (2002) criticises EU family-friendly policy because it fails to see that the way work is organised and separated from family is the main source of conflict for working parents; further, that this is a central factor shaping women's decisions about motherhood and employment participation. EU policy does not identify working mothers as citizens whose rights need to be protected, but as women workers. Guerrina argues that "this fails to encourage a redefinition of social structures of oppression that are particularly evident in the case of working mothers" (p. 56). Consequently, organisational structures are not recognised as the source of the problem and policy merely provides superficial protection, rather than real work-life reconciliation. This view is echoed within critiques of equal opportunities legislation, whereby the legislation advocates equal treatment for men and women, yet fails to recognise that "equal" treatment may not be appropriate, given men's and women's different labour market relationships and the fact that legislation derives from masculine organisational structures (Bock & James, 1992; Pateman, 1992; Callender, 1996). Furthermore, work and family continue to be viewed as separate spheres, whose interconnectedness is denied. As Taylor (2000) argues:

> The attempt to differentiate work from life in public policy making threatens to establish a false dichotomy between the two that obfuscates our attitude to the changing world of paid employment. We need to demystify what we are talking about if we hope to establish a sensible and realistic public policy agenda that can reconcile the conflicting pressures of the workplace and the home.
>
> (Taylor, 2000, p. 7)

Family responsibilities are not expected to impinge upon work commitments. However, the demands of employment and long-hours working continue to disrupt individuals', and especially fathers', participation in the domestic sphere. For those in professional occupations, it is frequently home life that becomes highly structured and determined by specific task allocations designed so as not to interfere with work, whereas "paid work has the character of more open and fluid time" (Lyon & Woodward, 2004, p. 207). Given the changing nature of paid work and the fact that individuals now carry out dual roles and are expected to do so, work and family can no longer be regarded as separate social areas and their "interspatiality" must be acknowledged.

Family-friendly policy should have two main aims. First, in practical terms, it should provide effective ways for men and women to carry out the demands of care and work, whilst still achieving an adequate quality of life. Secondly, it should address labour market inequality by providing individuals with the means both to participate in and progress within paid work, in spite of caring commitments. These objectives would be achieved primarily by a reorganisation of working practices, a re-evaluation of care and its value and place within society, and a recognition of the dual roles that individuals now perform. For instance, recent research by the Equal Opportunities Commission on discrimination against pregnant women highlights how dual care and work roles are still not recognised. Findings indicate that discriminatory practices against pregnant women continue to be a widespread problem (EOC, 2004b) Legislation may be designed with the aim of ensuring that women are protected. However, because there is no general acceptance that *women* now work as well as care, pregnancy and parenthood continue to be viewed as an unnecessary disruption to employment and business rather than a role that must now be recognised as *part* of the contemporary experience of paid work. Work needs to be reorganised to accommodate care, and care requires a more central focus, beyond its current marginal, invisible and feminised status.

Fiona Williams (2001) highlights the need for new approaches to these issues, arguing for an "ethics of care" which prioritises the need to care, rather than "care needs being fitted into the traditional requirements of work" (p. 488). Williams draws on the work of Pillinger (2000) to highlight the fact that making time and space the central focus enables the development of innovative and effective solutions to work-life balance and work-care conflicts. She argues that introducing new types of working time, such as "annualised hours, time banking and lifetime working hours, can give parents, and women in particular, more choices in negotiating work and care" (p. 473). Williams proposes a typology for work-life balance that is based around notions of time and space. These are: personal time and space; care time and space; and work time and space. Within Williams's formulation, rather than the over-prioritisation and separation of paid work, all three spheres are afforded similar degrees of importance, their interconnectedness is acknowledged, and "care" is allowed presence within the public sphere.

> A "care" culture in work organisations and in social and political organisations, such as Parliament, the trade unions and welfare services, would move away from male breadwinning times and cultures and prioritise the relational in people's lives... In addition, thinking across these areas allows us to prioritise the opportunities to give and receive care and to normalise responsibilities for giving care and support and needs for receiving care and support. (Williams, 2001, p. 489)

On the face of it, UK legislation does offer some time-based solutions to the issue of work-life balance for parents, via the flexible working request and the widening of flexible working within organisations. However, this is inconsistent across different industrial sectors and occupations. Moreover, as long as working long hours persists, it will undermine attempts at reconciling work and family responsibilities. In addition, the parental leave request needs to be more robust in terms of both awareness and entitlement. Parents need to know that this is a right to which they are entitled, designed to help them to manage their work and care responsibilities. There is still no real acknowledgement or acceptance of how people live their lives *across* the spheres of work and family. Such an acceptance of the true nature of the work-life balance is needed and should lead on to greater gender equity within the labour market, as care becomes more prominent and women are no longer expected discreetly to manage care around the margins of paid work.

References

Auer, M. (2002). The relationship between paid work and parenthood: A comparison of structures, concepts and developments in the UK and Austria. *Community, Work & Family, 5,* 203-18.

Ball, W. (2004, June). *Promoting gender equality?: Transforming childcare policies for mothers, fathers and children in Wales.* Paper presented at the International Conference on Work-Life Balance Across the Life Course, Centre for Research on Families and Relationships, University of Edinburgh.

Bang, H. P., Jensen, P. H., & Pfau-Effinger, B. (2000). Gender and European welfare states: Context, structure and agency. In S. Duncan & B. Pfau-Effinger (Eds.), *Gender, economy and culture in the European Union*. London: Routledge.

Blair, T, (2004, November 11). Full text: Tony Blair's speech on child care: The prime minister's speech to the Daycare Trust on November 11 2004 [Electronic version]. *The Guardian.*

Bock, G., & James, S. (Eds.). (1992). *Beyond equality and difference: Citizenship, feminist politics, and female subjectivity.* London: Routledge.

Bond, S., & Sales, J. (2001). Household work in the UK: An analysis of the British Household Panel Survey 1994. *Work, Employment and Society, 15,* 233-50.

Callender, C. (1996). Women and employment. In C. Hallett (Ed.), *Women and social policy: An introduction* (pp. 31-51). London: Prentice-Hall.

Coote, A. (2001). Feminism and the Third Way: A call for dialogue. In S. White (Ed.), *New Labour: The progressive future?* Basingstoke: Palgrave.

Council of the European Union (1993, November 23). *Council directive containing certain aspects of the organization of working time: Council directive 93/104/EC* [Electronic version]. Luxembourg: Office for Official Publications of the European Communities.

Council of the European Union (1996, June 3). *Framework agreement on parental leave: Council directive 96/34/EC* [Electronic version]. Luxembourg: Office for Official Publications of the European Communities.

Council of the European Union (1997, December 15). *Framework agreement on part-time working: Council directive 97/81/EC* [Electronic version]. Luxembourg: Office for Official Publications of the European Communities.

Court, G. (1995). *Women in the labour market: Two decades of change and continuity.* Brighton: Institute for Employment Studies.

Crompton, R. (2002). Employment, flexible working and the family. *British Journal of Sociology, 53,* 537-58.

Crompton, R., & Birkelund, G. E. (2000). Employment and caring in British and Norwegian banking: An exploration through individual careers. *Work Employment & Society, 14,* 331-52.

Crompton, R., Gallie, D., & Purcell, K. (1996). *Changing forms of employment: Organisations, skills and gender.* London: Routledge.

Crompton, R., & Harris, F. (1997). Women's employment and gender attitudes: A comparative analysis of Britain, Norway and the Czech Republic, *Acta Sociologica, 40,* 183-202.

Crompton, R., & Harris, F. (1998). Explaining women's employment patterns: 'Orientations to work' revisited. *British Journal of Sociology, 49,* 118-36.

Daly, M., & Lewis, J. (2000). The concept of social care and the analysis of contemporary welfare states. *British Journal of Sociology, 51,* 281-98.

Daycare Trust. (2001). *The price parents pay: Sharing the costs of childcare.* London: Author.

Dean, H. (2002). Business versus families: Whose side is New Labour on? *Social Policy and Society, 1,* 3-10.

Department of Social Security. (1998). *A new contract for welfare: The gateway to work.* London: Stationery Office.

Department of Trade and Industry. (2000). *Work & parents: Competitiveness and choice: a green paper.* London: Stationery Office.

Dex, S., (1987). *Women's occupational mobility: A lifetime perspective.* London: Macmillan.

Dex, S., & Scheibl F. (2002). *SMEs and flexible working arrangements.* Bristol: Policy Press.

Dex, S.. & Smith, C. (2002). *The nature and pattern of family-friendly employment policies in Britain.* Bristol: Policy Press/York: Joseph Rowntree Foundation.

Duncan, S. (2002). Policy discourses on 'reconciling work and life' in the EU. *Social Policy and Society, 1* (4), 305-314.

Duncan, S., Edwards, R., Reynolds, T., & Alldred, P. (2003). Motherhood, paid work and partnering: Values and theories. *Work, Employment and Society, 17* (2), 309-330.

Employment Relations Act: Elizabeth II, 1999, Chapter 26 (1999). London: Stationery Office.

Employment Act: Elizabeth II, 2002, Chapter 22 (2002). London: Stationery Office.

Equal Opportunities Commission. (2000). *The work-life balance.* Manchester: Author.

Equal Opportunites Commission. (2001). *The gender pay gap: A research review.* Manchester: Author.

Equal Opportunities Commission (2004a) *Parents in the workplace.* Manchester: Author.

Equal Opportunities Commission. (2004b) *Tip of the iceberg: Interim report of the EOC's investigation into discrimination against new and expectant mothers in the workplace.* Manchester: Author.

Eurostat [Statistical Office of the European Communities]. (2002). *European social statistics: Labour force survey results 2001: Data 2001.* Luxembourg: Office for Official Publications of the European Communities.

Evans, M., Eyre, J., Millar, J. & Sarre, S. (2003) *New Deal for Lone Parents: Second synthesis report for the national evaluation.* DWP, JAD, Sheffield: Research report 163.

Fagan, C. (2005). *Working-time preferences and work-life balance in the EU: some policy considerations for enhancing the quality of life.* Dublin: European Foundation for the Improvement of Living and Working Conditions.

Fagan, C., O'Reilly, J., & Rubery, J. (1999). Part-time work in the Netherlands, Germany and the UK: A challenge for relations between the sexes. *WSI Mitteilungen, 52,* 58-69.

Flexecutive. (2004). *Flexible working in the IT industry: Long-hours cultures and work life balance at the margins?: A report.* London: Department of Trade and Industry.

Flexibility.co.uk. (2004). *Flexible work a right? ... Not quite: We review the pros and cons of the "April laws" 2003.*

The Gendered Nature of Work-Life Balance
Retrieved October 17, 2004, from: http://flexibility.
co.uk/flexwork/general/flexible-right.htm.

Fraser, N. (1994). After the family wage: What do women want in social welfare? *Social Justice, 21*, 80-86.

Ginn, J., Street, D., & Arber, S. (Eds.). (2001). *Women, work, and pensions: International issues and prospects.* Buckingham: Open University Press.

Glass, J. L., & Estes, S. B. (1997). The family responsive workplace. *Annual Review of Sociology, 23*, 289-313.

Guerrina, R. (2002). Mothering in Europe: Feminist critique of European policies on motherhood and employment. *European Journal of Women's Studies, 9*, 49-68.

Gershuny, J., Godwin, L., and Jones, S. (1994). The domestic labour revolution: A process of lagged adaptation. In M. Anderson, F. Bechofer & J. Gershuny (Eds.), *The social and political economy of the household* (pp. 151 97). Oxford: Oxford University Press

Hakim, C. (1996). *Key issues in women's work: Female heterogeneity and the polarisation of women's employment.* London: Athlone Press.

Hakim, C. (2000). *Work-lifestyle choices in the 21st century: Preference theory.* Oxford: Oxford University Press.

Hall, M. (2001, April 28). Employers and unions respond to parental leave green paper. *EIROnline,* ID: UK0104125N. Retrieved July 1, 2008, from: http://www.eiro.eurofound.eu.int/2001/04/inbrief/uk0104125n.html

Hantrais, L. (2004). *Family policy matters: Responding to family change in Europe.* Bristol: Policy Press.

Himmelweit, S., & Sigala, M. (2002). *The welfare implications of mothers' decisions about work and childcare.* Leeds: ESRC Future of Work Programme.

Himmelweit, S., & Sigala, M. (2003). *Internal and external constraints on mothers' employment: Some implications for policy.* Leeds: ESRC Future of Work Programme.

Hochschild, A. R. (1997). *The time bind: When work becomes home and home becomes work.* New York: Metropolitan Books.

Hogarth, T., Daniel, W. W., Dickerson, A. P., Campbell, D. Winterbotham, D., & Vivian, D. (2003). *The business context to long hours working.* London: Department of Trade and Industry.

Hogarth, T., Hasluck. C., Pierre, G., Winterbotham, M., & Vivian, D. (2000). *Work-life balance 2000: Baseline study of work-life balance practices in Great Britain: Summary report.* London: Department for Education and Employment.

Jenkins, S. (2004). Restructuring flexibility: Case studies of part-time female workers in six workplaces. *Gender, Work and Organisation, 11,* 306-333.

Kodz, J., Harper, H., & Dench, S. (2002). *Work-life balance: Beyond the rhetoric*: Brighton: Institute for Employment Studies.

Kodz, J. et al., (2003). *Working long hours: A review of the evidence: Volume 1: Main report.* London: Department of Trade and Industry.

Land, H. (1980). The family wage. *Feminist Review, 6,* 55-77.

Land, H. (1999). The changing world of work and families. In S. Watson & L. Doyal (Eds.), *Engendering social policy* (pp. 12-29). Buckingham: Open University Press.

Lewis, J. (2001). The decline of the male breadwinner model: Implications for work and care. *Social Politics, 8,* 152-169.

Lewis, J., Mitchell, L., Woodland, S., Fell, R., & Gloyer, A. (2001). *Employers, lone parents and the work-life balance.* Sheffield: Employment Service Agency.

Lister, R. (1998). Vocabularies of citizenship and gender: The UK. *Critical Social Policy, 18,* 309-331.

Lister, R. (2000). To RIO via the Third Way: New Labour's 'welfare reform agenda'. *Renewal, 8,* 9-20.

Lister, R. (2003). Investing in the citizen-workers of the future: Transformations in citizenship and the state under New Labour. *Social Policy and Administration, 37,* 427-43.

Lyon, D., & Woodward, A. E. (2004). Gender and time at the top: Cultural constructions of time in high-level careers and homes. *European Journal of Women's Studies, 11,* 205-21.

Mansfield, P., & Collard, J. (1988). *The beginning of the rest of your life?: A portrait of newly-wed marriage.* Basingstoke: Macmillan.

McKie, L., Bowlby, S., & Gregory, S. (2001). Gender, caring and employment in Britain. *Journal of Social Policy, 30,* 233-58.

McKie, L., Gregory, S., & Bowlby, S. (2002). Shadow times: The temporal and spatial frameworks and experiences of caring and working. *Sociology, 36,* 897-924.

McRae, S. (1991). Occupational change after childbirth: Evidence from a national survey. *Sociology, 25,* 589-605.

Moss, P. (2001). *The UK at the crossroads: Towards an early years European partnership.* London: Daycare Trust.

Nickson, S. (2004). Legal q&a part-time workers: (Matthews v Kent & Medway Fire Authority). Retrieved August 18, 2009, from: http://www.accessmylibrary.com/com2/summary_02 86-12821532_ITM.

Office for National Statistics. (2003). *Labour force survey: Employment status by occupation and sex, April-June 2003.* London: Author.

Organisation for Economic Co-operation and Development. (2002). *Babies and bosses: Reconciling work and family life.* Paris: Author.

Parent-Thirion, A., Fernández Macías, E., Hurley, J., & Vermeylen, G. (2007). *Fourth European working conditions survey.* Luxembourg: Office for Official Publications of the European Community.

Pateman, C. (1992). Equality, difference, subordination: The politics of motherhood and women's citizenship. In G. Bock & S. James (Eds.), *Beyond equality and difference: Citizenship, feminist politics, and female subjectivity* (pp. 17-31). London, Routledge.

Pfau-Effinger, B. (1999). Welfare regimes and the gender division of labour in cross-national perspective: Theoretical framework and empirical results. In J.

Christiansen, P. Koistinen, & A. Kovalainen (Eds.), *Working Europe: Reshaping European employment systems.* Aldershot: Ashgate.

Pillinger, J. (2000) redefining work and welfare in Europe: New perspectives on work, welfare and time. In G. Lewis, S. Gerwitz & J. Clarke (Eds.), *Rethinking Social Policy.* London: Sage.

Pion Economics. (2003). *NWDA childcare provision review: final report.* Salford: Author.

Plantenga, J. (2002). Combining work and care in the polder model: An assessment of the Dutch part-time strategy. *Critical Social Policy, 22,* 53-71.

Rake, K. (2001). Gender and New Labour's social policies. *Journal of Social Policy, 30,* 209-31.

Rubery, J., & Fagan, C. (1995). Gender segregation in societal context. *Work, Employment and Society, 9,* 213-40.

Rubery, J., Horrell, S., & Burchell, B. (1994). Part-time work and gender inequality in the labour market. In A. M. Scott (Ed.), *Gender segregation and social change: men and women in changing labour markets* (pp. 205-34). Oxford: Oxford University Press.

Rubery, J., Smith, M., & Fagan, C. (1998). National working-time regimes and equal opportunities. *Feminist Economics, 4,* 71-101.

Squires, J., & Wickham-Jones, M. (2004). New Labour, gender mainstreaming and the Women and Equality Unit. *British Journal of Politics and International Relations, 6,* 81-98.

Statutory Instruments. (2000). *The part-time workers (prevention of less favourable treatment) regulations: Statutory instrument 2000, no. 1551* [Electronic version]. London: Stationery Office.

Taylor, R. (2000). *The future of work-life balance.* Swindon: Economic & Social Research Council.

Voet, R. (1998). *Feminism and citizenship.* London: Sage.

Walby, S., & Olsen, W. (2002). *The impact of women's position in the labour market on pay and implications for UK productivity.* London: Department of Trade and Industry, Women and Equality Unit.

Warde, A., & Hetherington, K. (1993). A changing domestic division of labour?: Issues of measurement and interpretation. *Work, Employment and Society, 7,* 23-45.

Warren, T. (2000, February 2). Women in low status part-time jobs: A class and gender analysis. *Sociological*

Research Online, 4 (4). Retrieved July 1, 2009, from: http://www.socresonline.org.uk/4/4/warren.html

Williams, F. (2001). In and beyond New Labour: Towards a new political ethics of care. *Critical Social Policy, 21,* 467-93.

Work and Family Act: Elizabeth II, 2006, Chapter 18 (2006). London: Stationery Office.

MATERNAL DRUG USE IN THE CONTEXT OF "FAMILY LIFE": ACCOUNTS OF MEXICAN-AMERICAN FEMALE INJECTING DRUG USERS AND THEIR CHILDREN

Catrin Smith

"The attitude is that you can't be a user and a mother. That's the stigma." (Female injecting drug user)

Introduction

It is estimated that more than six million children in the United States [US] live with a substance-abusing or substance-dependent parent (Office of Applied Studies, Substance Abuse and Mental Health Services Administration, 2003) and the potentially negative impact on children of problem substance use by parents has become an issue of increasing concern over recent years (Barnard & McKeganey, 2004). Here, it is suggested that children of problematic drug users often experience impaired parenting and are at risk of developing emotional and social problems, including drug dependence, later in life (Cuijpers, Langendoen & Bijl, 1999).

Little is known of the lives of children of problematic drug users (but see Gilligan, 2001; Barnard & Barlow, 2003; Bancroft, Wilson, Cunningham-Burley, Backett-Milburn & Masters, 2004) and even less is known abut the experience of living with problem drug use from the point of view of *both* the parent-cum-user and the child. Through an analysis of the accounts of female injecting drug users [IDUs] in San Antonio, Texas, and those of their children, this paper will consider the impact of maternal drug use on family life.

Fragmenting Family?

Research setting and methods

This paper draws upon the oral accounts of eight female IDUs and ten of their children, interviewed as part of a wider study of the social roles and relationships of Mexican-American female injecting heroin users in San Antonio, Texas (Smith, 2004; 2005)[1]. San Antonio is the ninth largest city in the US. It has a population of 1.4 million people, of which approximately 60% is Hispanic (mostly Mexican-American). San Antonio is a major site for drug trafficking because of its close proximity to the US-Mexico border and heroin use is endemic among the San Antonio Mexican-American population. Of the heroin users entering treatment programmes in San Antonio during 2002, 56% were Hispanic and approximately a third were women, most of whom were mothers (San Antonio Police Department, personal communication, 2004).

Mexican-American IDUs in the US tend to refer to themselves as *tecatos* rather than such terms as "junkies" or "smack-heads" (Ramos, Aguilar, Anderson & Caudillo, 1999). Ramos et al., in an examination of the culture of *tecatos*, suggested that, while the origin of the term is somewhat unclear, it is used to distinguish heroin and cocaine users from other substance users. They further highlight that the feminine of *tecato* is *tecata* (also see Andrade & Estrada, 2003). Throughout this paper, *tecata* will be used to refer to Mexican-American female injecting heroin users.

Tecatas (and by extension, their children) are something of a "hidden" or hard-to-reach population. They are often not included in research studies because they are seen to be more difficult to access than other populations (Ramos et al., 1999). The main study group of 32 *tecatas* aged between

[1] This research was supported by two separate grants from the British Academy, for which I am particularly grateful.

23 and 58 years was recruited, in the main, through personal contacts (Smith, 2005)[2]. "Snowball" or "network" sampling techniques were used, whereby the researcher started with an initial set of contacts and was passed on by them to others, who, in turn, referred others, and so on. Snowballing is particularly appropriate for the sampling of rare or "hidden" populations and is advantageous where those being studied are members of "deviant", vulnerable or stigmatised groups (McKeganey, 1990; Lee, 1993). During two intensive periods of fieldwork conducted in 2004-2005, knowledgeable active IDUs were sought out through visits to places such as bars, neighbourhood grocery stores, private homes, public housing apartments and prostitute strolling areas. Throughout this time, contact was kept with certain "high status" active IDUs, some of whom were drug dealers and "gatekeepers", to keep them informed about the purpose and progress of the study and to secure a certain amount of safety for the researcher.

All of the women recruited in the main study were active *tecatas* and all were mothers ($n=32$). All were poor, unemployed, and all were high school dropouts. Most of the women earned money through prostitution, stealing (mainly shoplifting), and committing burglaries. In all cases, other forms of substance use preceded injection drug use, with problematic substance use often beginning in response to a traumatic life event and often in adolescence. Injecting drug use histories ranged in length from two years to 25 years. Whilst most of the women said they were single, they often had a male partner, who on occasion they referred to as their common-law husband. In some cases,

---

[2] I acknowledge and thank Dr Reyes Ramos and Irma Aguilar for their invaluable help in locating respondents and for acting as "cultural consultants" to the project. Dr Reyes Ramos has extensive knowledge of *tecato* culture. Irma Aguilar is a recovering addict and is considered to be "high status" in the local San Antonio Mexican-American injecting drug user community.

the male partner was the father of their children. In all but three cases, the women lived in complex households where the occupants included children (biological and non-biological), as well as other family members, such as the women's siblings, grandchildren, cousins, niece, aunt, uncle, and, in one case, disabled mother. Most of the women were on probation or parole and only six had been in drug treatment.

In exploring the life experiences of the *tecatas* recruited for the study, the data collected included in-depth interviews as well as information derived from informal meetings and discussions. Throughout the fieldwork period, the women were met on many different occasions as the researcher became known to them and their families. All but three of the in-depth interviews took place in the women's homes, often with children and other family members close by (for example, family members would be in the kitchen whilst the interviews were taking place in small living rooms located off the kitchen). On many occasions, other members of the household talked openly to the researcher about their own experiences of substance using and criminal and/or other so-called risk behaviours. On one such occasion, the adult child of one of the respondents provided rich ethno-depictions of their childhood and of their experiences of problematic maternal drug use. The researcher was then referred to other female IDUs with older children and, in this manner, a second snowball sample of mothers and children emerged.

The study group of children consisted of four male and six female respondents aged 17-30 years and included those who had experienced problematic maternal drug use for a substantial period of their lives. Several of these respondents had criminal careers, and all but two reported current or previous problems with drugs or alcohol themselves. Four of the respondents were active injecting heroin users at the time of the interviews and two others described themselves as recovering IDUs. Several described being introduced to alcohol and/or illegal drugs by their parents or other family members, whilst others had first obtained such substances by stealing them from members of their household. Some reported that their mothers' heroin use had started after they themselves had started using. Four of the respondents had children themselves and one was also pregnant at the time of the interview. While some of the respondents were no longer living with their IDU mothers, all maintained regular contact, and the maternal home was often seen as the focal point for what one respondent described as "family business".

Mothers and children were interviewed separately (although invariably in the maternal home) and all the interviews were tape-recorded with the respondents' permission and were transcribed for qualitative analysis.

Findings: The "family lives" of tecatas and their children

The family has particular significance in Hispanic culture (Andrade & Estrada, 2003) and all the respondents talked in detail of the meaning of family and of their expectations as family members. Their narratives provided detailed ethno-depictions of their lives and of the ways in which they dealt with their circumstances. In their accounts, maternal substance use was often interwoven with other issues, such as poverty, violence, criminality, instability and, in the case of some of the children, their own substance use. All respondents provided rich descriptions of living with problematic drug use and of the impact of this on family life. In the accounts of the *tecatas* and their children, a number of key themes emerged.

Fragmenting Family?

1. Disruption and unpredictability

All respondents expressed a belief that close family relationships were important to them. However, their descriptions of "family life" were characterised by accounts of disruption, uncertainty, disappointment (for example, when expectations had not been met) and fear (of violence or about the welfare of family members). Respondents described how their households had been disturbed through, *inter alia*, frequent changes of address (often to escape from violence and often without much warning), changes in the make-up of the family unit as different people came and went, children being looked after by relatives and, in a few instances, by state agencies, and periods of mother-child separation (through, for example, maternal imprisonment). The unpredictable nature of injecting drug use itself was also a key theme in the accounts, as the following extracts from three of the children of *tecatas* illustrate:

> I mean, your Mom is meant to be the heart of the family. She is the one that keeps everything together. She is the protector and the carer. The neck without which the head would topple. And, on good days, she [mother] is all these things. But on bad days, man, it's all over the place.

> My memory is of her being there and then not being there. No day was the same, up and down. Anything could happen and that was the way it was.

> You know, you just wanted things to be normal, like normal families. Just once I wanted to be able to act like a normal kid, to bring friends home. But you never knew what sort of state she would be in or even if she would be here, whether or not she'd been arrested or worse. That was my life.

Barnard and McKeganey (2004) have highlighted the extent to which problematic drug use is characterised by periods

114

of controlled drug intake and relative stability, and periods of relapse, escalating drug use and instability. All of the respondents in this study described the chaotic, yo-yoing nature of drug dependency and all pointed to the ways in which this, at times, undermined family functioning and the stability of the household. The following excerpts from four *tecatas* illustrate this:

> When it [heroin] takes hold of you, it becomes everything, everything. It takes over your life. Some nights I'll do anything for a fix. I'll be out all night, you know, trying to score and everything else has to wait. The house will be a mess. I'll forget to eat or to get the kids sorted. It's not a nice way to be, I can tell you.

> The times when I have the devil [heroin] under control, you know, or I have plenty of drugs, then I can be normal, be a normal Mom to my kids. But when it is in control of me … At those times, you don't want to know me. I don't want to know me.

> To be honest, life just depends on the drugs. So, there is no typical day. It is just up and down. You might not get the money. You might get arrested. You might get into a fight. Who can say.

> Anything could have happened to the kids when they were younger and I probably wouldn't have been in any fit state to sort them out. I mean she [daughter] nearly died when she was about four or five. She nearly drowned in the river up near Gruene. And where was I? I was out of it. Her brother had to jump in and drag her out.

During periods of escalating maternal drug use and instability, children may be particularly vulnerable, with their needs taking second place to those imposed by the drug problem (Hogan & Higgins, 2001; McKeganey, Barnard & McIntosh, 2002; Barnard & McKeganey, 2004). Children may be at risk of not having their basic social, emotional and physical needs met as their family lives become chaotic and uncertain and everyday routines such as mealtimes become subsumed by the preoccupation with drugs.

> There was never much food in the house. Sometimes, when she'd got her cheque or had pulled a date [prostituted], there would maybe be some food or she would bring something back for us from the diner. Most of the time there would be nothing, just some scraps of bread if we were lucky.

While some of the respondents could recount times when the impact of maternal drug use on family life was minimal (see also Hogan & Higgins, 2001) and others described periods of relative stability (whether drug free or thanks to a methadone-maintenance programme), the predominance of drugs in the women's and children's lives was a salient feature of all accounts. For instance, in the accounts of the children we can see recollections of a childhood dominated by drugs (see also Barnard & Barlow, 2003):

> One of my first memories is of scoring drugs. I was only small and I can remember her going out and she took me with her. That was really the way our life was. It was all about the drugs. Everything else was forgotten about. Some days there would be food, if perhaps she'd got some money. But other days …

> The only routine to speak of was to do with drugs. Everything revolved around drugs.

When asked about the effect of maternal drug use on the quality of their relationships with their mothers, most of the children spoke about the uncertainties and inconsistencies associated with problematic drug use. In particular, the children recounted a sense of insecurity about, for example, maternal absences (often for days at a time) and of their feelings that their mothers were often "not there" for them, literally and metaphorically. Here, the children often pointed to times when they had felt "let down", hurt or rejected by their mothers or when they felt that their mothers had been inconsistent in their affections. This said, all of the children interviewed felt that their drug-using mothers had tried their best for them. Many of them blamed others for their mother's drug use (for example, boyfriends) and there was a tendency to accord their mothers something of a victim status (also see Bancroft et al., 2004). The following excerpt from the son of one *tecata* illustrates this:

> I mean, man, she's had it tough. It's not been easy for her and she tries her best to be here for us. She does. But, you know, my Mom, she's hooked. She's got a problem. Her man [boyfriend] started her with it. She was clean and then she got together with this guy and now she is hooked and with that I tell you everything. He got locked up and she got in the medicine [methadone]. But he got out two months ago and she started using again with him. She got hooked again.

2. *Mother and* tecata: *Role management and role conflict*

The women interviewed in this study are, of course, not *only tecatas*. They are also *inter alia* mothers, family members, IDU network members, prostitutes, drug dealers, parolees, and/or probationers. They perform their high-risk behaviour in the context of the various roles they play (see also Ramos et al., 1999). The women talked in detail about their role as mothers and of the ways in which they attempted to manage this alongside their other roles, as the following extracts highlight:

> I may be a user. But I love my kids and I am a good mother to them. But I am struggling. It's hard, you know, to sort out all these things. I'm always running around because the younger children are in school and I have to be home when they get here. I want to stop the drugs but, what can I tell you, I'm hooked. So, there's the job of getting money for that, the kids, my family. It's hard work, you know?

> It's a strange thing, but when people know you are a user that is all they see. That is all they want to see. They don't seem to understand that, yes, we may be drug addicts, but we are also people. We have lives and families and even jobs. I have always tried to be there for

my kids and my family. I sell [drugs] and so I am a dealer. But I sell to pay the bills and to get food for the kids as well as to get the fix.

I try to keep all this [prostitution and drug dealing activities] from the kids and from my mother. I work [sell] from another place and keep my gear there. It can be hard to keep all these bits of my life straight, so that you don't mess things up. It's tiring going here and there and trying to get my mother [who is disabled] sorted and comfortable and to be home when the girls are home. I can't leave them alone.

I tell you that's why I have to work [prostitute]. To pay for things, the food, the rent. You know, people see me there – selling my sorry ass – and they think it's just about the fix. But, it's more for the sake of the kids than for the fix.

Here, we can see the potential for role conflict, as the role of mother and parent may be subsumed by the role of *tecata*. All of the women told of their efforts to be "good" mothers, whilst recognising that, at times, they were unable to maintain this front owing to a preoccupation with drugs (see also Schuler, Nair, Black & Kettinger, 2000). The women described the "job" of negotiating a drug career (which can be financially draining), whilst also participating in family and other activities. Here, they often needed to resort to criminal means to support both their habit *and* their children.

The women interviewed also talked about their attempts to hide their drug use from their children (by, for example, always wearing long sleeves to hide track marks, hiding drugs and injecting equipment, locking themselves in the bathroom or only injecting when children were out or asleep). In contrast, the children interviewed revealed that they had often become aware of maternal drug use long before their mothers thought they had (see also Barnard & Barlow, 2003). This is highlighted in the following two excerpts. The first is from a female IDU and the second is from her son. Together, the excerpts illustrate the unpredictable nature of maternal drug use, as well as the way in which a sudden change in circumstances can make individuals re-think and/or alter their definitions of reality[3].

> *Mother:* I always work hard to hide it from the kids. I hide my track marks because I don't want to give a bad example. I never shoot up around them. When I go out to work [hustling and prostitution], I tell them that I have to go and do something, some job. And the times when I have plenty of drugs or when I am in control, things are OK, normal. But, I have to admit to you that there are times when things are wild and out of it and the kids make life hard. One day I was ill [experiencing withdrawal] and I told the kids that I was sick and not to bother me. Well, they went crazy. Fighting with each other, what can I tell you? And I was so sick. I had no control to stop them. But I don't do it where they can see it. Like today I have got her [daughter] in the other room because I don't want her to hear what we say. You know my son knows, but the others don't. I think.

> **Son:** You never know what to expect. There's no typical day. You can't say that maybe next Saturday everything will be OK, we can go to the park or something, have barbecue, act like a normal family. You just don't know what to expect from one day to the next. On good days, maybe when she's scored and got some money, we'll have food in the house. On bad days, there might just be some chips, nothing else, and she'll be in a mess.

He continues:

> She tries to hide it from us but…. She knows I know, but she thinks that the others don't. But they are not fools. I found out when she was busted. Man, I felt so stupid. I didn't know for a long time. She hides it well. My uncle told me. He's a *tecato* too. Man, everybody is one. I wouldn't believe him when he said what she was doing and that she is shoplifting. But then she got busted. She never told me

---

[3] Schutz (1967) points to the existence of multiple realities and suggests that people only question their definition of social reality when it is contradicted by some unexpected event.

she was using, but then I noticed more and more, her behaviour, you know. She spends a long time in the bathroom or she locks herself in the bedroom. Man, it's there when you look for it. I just couldn't see it before.

For some of the children, maternal injecting drug use pre-dated their birth or had begun when they were very young. For others, their mothers' drug usage developed later and was often associated with other sources of household stress: for example, the death of a family member, the imprisonment of a family member, revelations of sexual abuse of a family member, an injury or the development of long-term health problems. Whilst only one of the children reported having been told directly of their mother's heroin use, all could recall how they first became aware of there being a problem and all could cite occasions where some unexpected event led to a phenomenological shift in thinking about their mother.

I walked in on her. She was there with the syringe sticking out of her arm. I remember it clearly. I was about seven. That's the first time and then she didn't bother to hide it after that. She started doing it in front of me.

Everything was OK until he [father] died [of an overdose]. I look back on it and it's like everything was good before then. When he died, she went crazy. That's when it all started really.

When I was about 15, she [mother] started getting into it heavily and that's when I realised it was smack. It was around that time that my brother got jail, my sister was molested by some guy in the neighbourhood and there was a whole lot of mad stuff going on. She got into it heavy at that time.

She's got a problem. You know that she is a *tecata* and that she is out there hustling. And she's trying to hide it and all that shit. I've told her there's no use in pretending. I found out when the police caught her with a gun. They caught her with a gun and they locked her up.

3. Role reversal and the nature of the mother-child relationship

There is no doubt that maternal drug use can affect the *quality* of relationships between mothers and children (Kandel, 1990). It also has the potential to affect the *nature* of those relationships, as problems with parenting lead to a degree of role reversal. The lives of the children interviewed had, to a greater or lesser extent, been affected by their mothers' immersion in drugs and their subsequent responsibilities for looking after themselves, their mothers, other family members and the household. Respondents described how, even from an early age, they often had to become responsible for the care of others, as the following excerpts illustrate:

> Who else was there? She [mother] was out of it more often than not. So I was left to look after everything else. When she's in that state, she can't even look after herself, let alone the rest of us.

> You know your mom is supposed to look after you, care for you, see that you are OK. But for us, it was the other way round. We had to look after her and whoever she was with at the time. It was like we were the adults and they were the little ones.

> On one occasion she just disappeared for a week and I had the job of sorting the family and everything else out.

> She runs around with *lecatos*, injecting themselves. She doesn't eat or sleep, the house is a mess. There will be people calling at the house at all times because she deals from here. There will be parties at the house. And I usually end up having to take care of things. I have to do all that.

The burden of responsibility placed on children was also recognised in the accounts of their mothers, as the following observations show:

> She had to grow up too quick. She had to look after the house, the others, all of us really. If the truth be known, she was the one who

kept things together when she was growing up. She was really the Mom to the others and, if the truth be known, to me as well.

He [son] had to become the man of the house, you know? He had to do everything for himself and his brother.

Several of the children interviewed described how they looked after, not only the practical needs of their mothers or siblings, but also their emotional needs. For example, one respondent highlighted the way in which she felt that her mother had become emotionally dependent upon her:

She needs me. It is as simple as that. I don't just mean that she needs me to do the cooking or cleaning or to take care of the others. I think she would fall apart if I wasn't around to talk to her and to listen to her. Sometimes, when she's sick, I have to go to her. Or she'll wake me up in the middle of the night because she wants to talk. There is no one else, you see.

Here, we can see a qualitative shift in the nature of the relationship between mother and child, away from the familial and more towards one resembling something of companionship. The effect of maternal drug use on the nature of the mother-child relationship was also evidenced in some of the children's accounts of their exposure to criminality and of their own substance use (see also McKeganey et al., 2002):

Sometimes we shoot up together and we share [syringes]. I always used to share with my brother and sister and my boyfriend as well. And sometimes I think, "That's my Mom fixing".

She [mother] only started using after I started when I was about 13. I am trying to leave the habit, but I'm hooked. And I know that she is not trying to do me any harm, but she is addicted and sometimes she has it [heroin] with her. So I can buy it from her, from my own mother. I'm trying to kick, but she is here so the temptation is there, even in the house. If it is not her, it is my brother. It is hard now that I want to stop.

> I'd go with her when she went out to sell [drugs] or steal. I'd seen the inside of a jail before I was four [visiting family members]. I was with my Mom once when she got busted and I had to wait for someone to come down to the police place and get me. Things like that.

> Sometimes we work [prostitute] together to get money for fixing. Some guys – the dates – like to screw a mother and daughter.

When questioned on their feelings as to the nature of the mother-child relationship, respondents had conflicting views (see also Bancroft et al., 2004). Many of the women interviewed reported guilt at putting their children in a position of care and of exposing them to a lifestyle characterised by risk:

> She has to do everything and I do feel bad about that. That's no way to grow up. She should be out enjoying herself, but she's here looking after me and her brothers.

> It's not right that he has to do all this. And look at him. He has his own problems too. I feel so, so sorry when I think about the way he is, the drugs, the life he has had to lead.

> My children have had no real life to speak of. It is a disgusting way to live and they have seen more in their lives than is right.

> I do worry about it. I used to sell from the house. But there was this time when some men came to the house and I thought they wanted to do some deal. But they were carrying [armed with guns] and all hell broke loose. The kids were screaming. It wasn't nice for them. I knew then that it was enough and I sell from that other place now.

For some of the children (and, particularly, the females), the caring for others seemed to be a powerful part of their self-identity. For others, the family dynamics around maternal drug use were so ingrained into their everyday lives and experiences that they found it difficult to reflect upon or to imagine a different set of roles and relationships. For others still, there was a certain amount of resentment and anger about their role as carers and/or about their exposure to criminality and drug culture. For example, the daughter of one *tecata* explained that, whilst she loved her mother, she felt bitter about the fact that she had become responsible for the care of other family members. She felt that she had missed out on her education and social life as a consequence and was frequently overwhelmed with concern about the welfare of her mother and siblings. Others, similarly, discussed the loss of their childhood, as the following quote highlights:

> I do feel like my childhood was taken away. When I was growing up I didn't know any different. That was life. That was the way it was. But now that I've got kids myself, I look back on my life and wonder where it all went and, yes, sometimes I do get angry. Kids should be able to grow up without all that. I don't think it is right that kids have to grow up so soon. I mean, I was all grown up when I was seven. I didn't have any choice. I was the mom. I had to be.

4. Maternal reputation and stigma

Andrade and Estrada (2003, p. 1141) argue that the "reputation of the family is held as sacrosanct" in Hispanic culture, where great measures are taken to protect the reputation of the family from "the potential gossip borne out of publicly airing out problems and conflicts, which is a sign of weakness". They suggest that the fear of "what others will have to say" looms large and has particular implications for female drug users (2003, p. 1142). Whilst injecting heroin use is widespread in the San Antonio Mexican-American population, the stigma that surrounds drug dependency and the need to maintain the "family secret" were key themes in the narratives of the women and children interviewed. For example, one mother recounts her concerns about participating in a drug intervention programme:

Maternal Drug Use in the Context of "Family Life"

I have told you this before. I do need some help. But I don't want to go to my appointment. I am worried that someone sees me, sees me at my appointment. They'll know that I am using. So I don't go.

Both mothers and children talked about their reluctance to speak openly about maternal drug use for fear of public and cultural censure. Where maternal drug use predated their birth, or where it began when they were young, the children talked about having been aware from quite an early age of the need for secrecy. All of the children conveyed a sense of complicity in having to conceal their mother's use. For example, the son of one *tecata* described how he kept his mother's drug use a secret from others (including the police and state agencies):

Just say nothing. That was the rule. If anyone asks you anything, just say nothing, act dumb. It was like if anyone found out or the police asked you, or teachers asked you, there might be big trouble.

Some of the children discussed the stigma of having had to be looked after by others (owing, for example, to their mother's imprisonment). Others expressed embarrassment and, to a lesser extent, shame at their mother's drug use and described various strategies to cover up their mother's behaviour. In their efforts not to reveal the problem (such as not attending school, not letting people into the house, not socialising with other people), these children depict a life characterised by social isolation and exclusion:

I just never went out for fear that someone would ask about her, you know what I mean? So, I would just sit in and if we did go out, I would always be thinking about who might be watching us, what they might be thinking.

People are always throwing it in my face. You know, that she is a junkie. That is why I don't hang out around the neighbourhood any more and why I want to move from round here. People just throwing it back at me.

Bancroft et al. (2004) note that the stigma that surrounds parental drug use is often more acute with mothers than it is with fathers. This is because parenting tends to be seen as the preserve of women (see also Hogan, 1998) and a low, irrevocable status is accorded to the woman drug addict (Nurco, Wegner & Stephenson, 1982). Women's drug use challenges traditional female stereotypes and notions of appropriate femininity, and the female user represents femininity misplaced, defied and defiled. Specifically, women drug users embody women who have rejected their femininity. As such, they are "non-women" (Perry, 1979).

Ettorre (1992) illustrates this clearly in her analysis of women and heroin. She argues that, in the hierarchy of drugs, heroin is seen as a particularly masculine drug (as opposed to psychotropic drugs, such as Prozac, which are seen to be particularly feminine). She argues that, because of women's social positioning, the boundaries of behaviour are more narrowly defined for women than for men. Because of this, the consequences of transgressing these social boundaries for women drug users are more severe. In this sense, regardless of why women take drugs, these women are thought to have polluted their bodies and spoiled their identities as women. Certainly, the women interviewed in this study recognised the impact of their addiction on their identities as women and, in particular, their identities as mothers.

> I think that there is a double standard here. The man who uses is seen in one way and the woman is seen in another way. The woman is seen as trash, as dirty and as the lowest form of life. And if she is a mother, God help her.

> There is a stigma about being a user. But if you are a mother and a user then that is much, much worse. It is as if you cannot be a mother *and* a user. I know this.

The incompatibility between the social expectations of motherhood and the actuality of drug addiction was also evident in the narratives of the children. For example, the daughter of one *tecata* discussed her desires for her mother to get clean. However, she recognised that this was not easy, given the persistent negative imagery surrounding maternal drug use:

> I want her to kick [the habit] but, what can I tell you, it is hard for her. I want her to go to the free medicine [methadone] place that you told me about. But she worries about what people will say if she goes. She does not want people to know and she thinks that people will throw it back at her. There are people who have the attitude. They think, "that woman is a mother and look at her, she is hooked, she uses the needle". So, she cannot help herself to kick. She cannot get the help she needs because of this attitude.

The decision to conceal their habit, however, is in direct conflict to any harm reduction strategies in this community (Andrade & Estrada, 2003). Here, gender and cultural imperatives and the need to suffer in silence may well interfere with the potential for drug prevention and intervention or treatment. Mexican-American female IDUs may decide not to apply for drug-user treatment for fear of condemnation. For those who do, they often encounter oppressive and gendered practices in the drug treatment system, a system designed for the male majority (Ettorre, 1992; Ramos et al., 1999).

Discussion

This paper describes something of the experience of family life in the context of maternal drug use (and *vice versa*) from the perspective of mothers and their children. It points to the all-encompassing, yet unpredictable, nature of problematic drug use and how it can come to dominate all aspects of everyday life. For all of the mothers and children interviewed, the nature of maternal injecting drug use and of heroin addiction was such that it was very hard to avoid it affecting the dynamics, relationships, positions and roles within the family. As their accounts suggest, maternal drug use could, and did have the capacity to impact upon "normal" family functioning. Nonetheless, family relationships remained important to all respondents.

The focus on the nature of familial relationships in the context of female injecting drug use is important. It is clear that the drug-using, criminal and sexual activities of *tecatas* are structured in relation to other life activities. However, these women are not just IDUs. They must maintain the roles of mother, partner, relative, and so forth, whilst also maintaining a drug career. They perform their high-risk behaviour in terms of the various roles they play (Ramos et al., 1999). Similarly, the children's relationships with their mothers are framed by the roles they play (and which may include the role of carer). Therefore, it is important to consider how mothers and children construct a relationship within the context of these various roles, how they define social reality, and how different definitions of reality often clash.

The findings of this small-scale study have implications for further research and for the development of relevant intervention services. The mothers interviewed all described their attempts to manage their drug use in terms of their parental role. This role was also, somewhat ironically, seen as a barrier to help-seeking. Culture and gender expectations require women to conform to social imperatives or, at least, to appear to be doing so. When female IDUs break with these "unspoken rules" (Andrade & Estrada, 2003, p. 1152), they are seen as failures. Hence, they suffer in silence. Similarly, the voices of the children of problem drug users are effectively silenced. Further work is required to develop the means of enabling female IDUs and their children to express their thoughts and feelings about their circumstances without fear of public censure. An understanding of the commonsense knowledge that they use to define their situation and social relationships (that is, listening to their voices) may help to provide a meaningful framework for the development of culturally relevant intervention strategies.

Finally, there is little doubt that maternal drug use impacts upon children's lives in many ways. For example, academic difficulties are common amongst the children of problematic drug users and many go on to have criminal careers and substance use and/or mental health problems themselves. However, it is difficult to think about this impact in isolation from other issues. Maternal drug use is interspersed with other complex psycho-social problems and it is often difficult to disentangle the specific contribution of drugs towards the likelihood of poor child outcomes. Not all of the children interviewed in this study felt that maternal drug use had had an impact on their lives irrespective of other factors, such as poverty, child abuse, and the fear of, and actuality of, violence. Frequent references were made in all the respondents' accounts to the use of drugs as a means for dealing with emotional upheaval and pain. Here, it is suggested that maternal drug use may be an *effect* rather than a specific *cause* of the problem and that effective intervention strategies will be those that recognise that it is the social and cultural context in which "high risk" behaviours occur that informs an individual's very definition of risk.

References

Andrade, R., and Estrada, A. L. (2003). Are Hispana IDUs *tecatas*?: Reconsidering gender and culture in Hispana injection drug use. *Substance Use and Misuse, 38,* 1133-58.

Bancroft, A., Wilson, S., Cunningham-Burley, S., Backett-Milburn, K., and Masters, H. (2004). *Parental drug and alcohol misuse. Resilience and transition among young people.* York: Joseph Rowntree Foundation.

Barnard, M. A., and Barlow, J. (2003). Discovering parental drug dependence: Silence and disclosure. *Children and Society, 17,* 45-56.

Barnard, M. A., and McKeganey, N. P. (2004). The impact of parental problem drug use on children: What is the problem and what can be done to help?, *Addiction, 99,* 552-9.

Cuijpers, P., Langendoen, Y., and Bijl, R. (1999). Psychiatric disorders in adult children of problem drinkers: Prevalence, first onset and comparison with other risk factors, *Addiction, 94,* 1489-98.

Ettorre, E. (1992). *Women and substance use.* Basingstoke: Macmillan.

Gilligan, R. (2001). *Promoting resilience: A resource guide on working with children in the care system.* London: British Agencies for Adoption and Fostering.

Hogan, D. M. (1998). Annotation: The psychological development and welfare of children of opiate and cocaine users: Review and research needs. *Journal of Child Psychology and Psychiatry, 39,* 609-20.

Hogan, D. M., and Higgins, L. (2001). *When parents use drugs: Key findings from a study of children in the care of drug-using parents.* Dublin: Trinity College Dublin, Children's Research Centre.

Kandel, D. B. (1990). Parenting styles, drug use, and children's adjustment in families of young adults. *Journal of Marriage and the Family, 52,* 183-96.

Lee, R. M. (1993). *Doing research on sensitive topics.* London: Sage.

McKeganey, N. P. (1990). Drug abuse in the community: Needle-sharing and the risks of HIV infection. In S. Cunningham-Burley and N. P. McKeganey (Eds.), *Readings in Medical Sociology* (pp. 113-37). London: Tavistock/Routledge.

McKeganey, N. P., Barnard, M. A., and McIntosh, J. (2002). Paying the price for their parents' addiction: Meeting the needs of the children of drug-using parents. *Drugs: Education, Prevention and Policy, 9,* 233-46.

Nurco, D. N., Wegner, N., and Stephenson, P. (1982). Female narcotic addicts: Changing profiles. *Journal of Addiction and Health, 3,* 62-105.

Office of Applied Studies, Substance Abuse and Mental Health Services Administration (2003). *The NHSDA report: Children living with substance-abusing or substance-dependent parents.* Rockville, MD: Author.

Perry, L. (1979). *Women and drug use: An unfeminine dependency.* London: Institute for the Study of Drug Dependence.

Ramos, R., Aguilar, I., Anderson, M., and Caudillo, V. (1999). *Tecatas:* An ethnotheoretical look at Mexican American female injecting drug users. *Substance Use & Misuse, 34,* 2015-55.

Schuler, M. E., Nair, P., Black, M. M., and Kettinger, L. (2000). Mother-infant interaction: Effects of a home intervention and ongoing maternal drug use. *Journal of Clinical Child Psychology, 29,* 424-31.

Schutz, A. (1967). *Collected papers, 1: The problem of social reality* (M. Natanson, Ed.). (2nd ed.). The Hague: Nijhoff.

Smith, C. (2004). *An ethnographic study of female injecting drug users in San Antonio, Texas: Developmental phase.* Final report (unpublished) presented to the British Academy.

Smith, C. (2005). *An ethnographic study of female injecting drug users in San Antonio, Texas.* Final report (unpublished) presented to the British Academy.

"AND STAY OUT !": HOODS AND PARAMILITARISED YOUTH: EXILING AND PUNISHMENT BEATINGS

Katy Radford

The paper was prompted by research carried out in Hydebank Young Offenders' Centre (Radford, Hamilton & Jarman, 2005). Additional research is drawn from work carried out in the Shankill Road area of Belfast with young loyalists who came from families in which one or more members had received paramilitary warnings, beatings and exclusions.

During the research period, Northern Ireland's devolved government collapsed. It had originally been set up after the Peace Agreement of 1998. The Stormont Assembly did not sit again for several years until after the St Andrews Agreement of 2007, with direct rule coming from Westminster during that time. One of the principal sticking blocks throughout this period concerned policing, which *de facto* had implications for community policing and informal justice systems (Jarman, 2006).

Since then, changes within Northern Ireland's policy and political landscapes have seen communities strive for a future shared rather than divided. To that end, the formation of a Commission for Victims and Survivors, as well as a growth in Community Restorative Justice programmes, have added new commentators and opportunities into the mix (Byrne & Monaghan, 2009) and for those interested in considering these areas further, the catalogue of work by Kieran McEvoy and Harry Mika might be considered.

Fragmenting Family?

Introduction

The history of the political struggle in Northern Ireland has left a number of tragic legacies in communities, including children being inducted from an early age into a culture that is tolerant of violence. This exposure to violence and the legacy of civil and political unrest has resulted in some young people drawing on negative coping strategies, such as alcohol and drug misuse (Chamberlain, 2001). This process is now prevalent across many communities.

The conflict in Northern Ireland has been a continual focus of attention, with the lens of the international media and the pens of academics aimed at different aspects of the brutal results of the armed struggle between the state and paramilitary forces. O'Mailoain's register of conflict-related studies on Northern Ireland notes that, in 1993 alone, there were some 605 projects being researched. In addition to these academic works, there are many popular explorations specifically of loyalist paramilitarism (Boulton, 1973; Nelson, 1984; Dillon, 1989; Bruce, 1992; Crawford, 1999) or Republicanism (Coogan, 1980; Beresford, 1987; of Protestant agitation (Anderson, 1994, Shirlow & McGovern 1997), and of general sectarianism (Boyd, 1987). A review of the legacy and cost in human terms of sectarian violence is available in the chronology of McKittrick et al. (1999).

The paramilitary punishment of young people perpetuated by those from within their own communities has been the subject of much academic literature (Byrne, 2004; and, for an overview, see Feenan, 2002, p. 41). Much of this work focuses on the value of developing appropriate mechanisms of mediation between victims and offenders, whilst acknowledging the widespread approval in Northern Ireland of restorative and non-retributive justice systems (Criminal Justice Review Group, 2000, p. 203). This locates the discourse of punishment and

134

exclusions firmly within the perspective of a criminological framework, with particular attention paid to the matter when the focus is community based (McEvoy & Mika, 2002b). The history of informal and restorative justice as a proactive community response to offending behaviour has been part of an Irish system of governance that pre-dates the Brehon laws and was revived in the 1960s.

For some, a reliance on community-based restorative justice programmes as a form of internal community policing provides a welcome extension of vigilantism. This can be identified with the legacy and perpetuation of systems in which there is a deep-rooted lack of confidence in aspects of the criminal justice system. Some commentators have placed the debate within a framework that concentrates on how communities struggle to respond to anti-social behaviour and crime, particularly in Republican areas, in the absence of consensual policing (Connolly, 1997; Conway, 1997, p. 109; McEvoy & Mika, 2002a, p. 62, Jarman 2006). For others, this reliance is identified as a potentially novel form of community development that permits alternative initiatives, so as to legitimise the reintegration of politically-motivated activists, offenders and ex-prisoners into prominent and high-status roles within local communities, via systems of restorative justice co-managed by the statutory agencies (Winston, 1997). A useful historical contextualisation and summary of the principal debates from which current initiatives have begun to emerge can be found in Monaghan (2002).

Other commentators have focused more deliberately on the brutal aspects of informal justice systems, working from the position that there is a myriad of ways in which self-appointed operators of informal justice systems function outside the tacit and acceptable boundaries of the communities that they claim to represent. These analyses point towards the physical and emotional damage perpetuated on the accused or on those who have been inducted into perpetrating brutal atrocities (see Knox, 2001; Knox & Monaghan, 2002). For those who accept the latter position, the realities of the processes and practices of some informal justice systems appear to be less about articulating community cohesion in the face of unacceptable legitimate systems, and more about the physical and psychological intimidation of the communities own deviant and marginalised people.

Whatever the dichotomies thrown up by these competing positions, the voices and experiences of young people who have, either directly or indirectly through their families, experienced punishment beatings and exiling are seldom heard. However, they can provide us with a lens through which to view aspects of the process in action. Consequently, what is of particular relevance here is the acknowledgement that the least palatable aspect of the restorative process is to be found in its gaps. This will involve looking at the unsuccessful cases: those that do not engage with the process of mediation between victims and offenders and that result in young people themselves and their families receiving threats, beatings, shootings, and exilings, in the name of informal justice.

Case Study

Brian is 17. He has been in a juvenile justice centre for five months, for a robbery. Prior to his incarceration, he lived for six months on a housing estate in Belfast with his birth family. He walks with a limp, because of a punishment shooting that he received some months before from another paramilitary group, for "stroking things out of a car shop".

He says, "… like I didn't know it was owned by the XXX".

He has been the focus of attention of both the formal and the informal justice systems operating in Northern Ireland for many years. "I was always getting chased and lifted by the peelers since I was a kid."

On the subject of paramilitaries, he says: "They've come in and wrecked my house when I wasn't there, looking for drugs, and I got a beating once for joyriding that was so bad that I couldn't go out of the house for days." Brian says he still has flashbacks and attributes his insomnia to this incident.

It is as a result of his earlier involvement with the paramilitaries that his family has moved three times in as many years. "First I was put under curfew, then I was told I had 24 hours to get out. I was out for a couple of weeks and then I wanted to come back in and that was OK, but then I was put out again."

Brian now lives only half a mile from where his baby daughter and previous girlfriend live, but he is unable to visit them on that estate because of a paramilitary exclusion order that has been placed on him.

He has a friend who has been on one community restorative justice programme and both acknowledge that a key benefit was that, "When he tried to come back in again to the estate, he was put on a programme and that stopped him getting a beating. They work with paramilitaries and work with the housing executive and all. They work with everyone, so they do. If you go to them and say that you're under paramilitary threat and all, it gets you a house quicker that way, so it's a good project and I'm going to go down and see them once I get out of here, because they can find out who's got the threat lifted and who's got it still on them."

He remains an optimist: "Last time I was in here, I couldn't get on a training scheme 'cos they only take you from 16, but they'll get me on one this time."

***

At this stage, it may be useful to move away from the theoretical context to get a sense of the scale of the practical issues. Figure 1 shows the total referrals of under-17 year-olds to the crisis intervention agency, Base2, from 1998 to 2003. This is the main route recognised by the statutory service providers for enabling those under paramilitary threat to be relocated. During 2003, this NIACRO-funded project dealt on average with two under-17 year-olds who had been threatened by paramilitary groups every week. Table 1 provides a breakdown of people forced to relocate owing to paramilitary threats and intimidation. (Source of the tables: Base2 Annual Statistics, 2002).

Figure 1

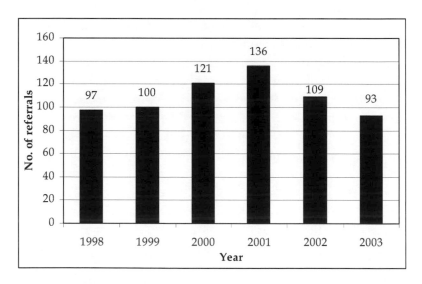

Table 1

Year	1995	1996	1997	1998	1999	2000	2001	2002	2003
Relocation outside Northern Ireland	55	126	81	88	57	45	39	60	57
Relocation within Northern Ireland	76	128	198	247	199	278	458	471	287
Total	131	254	279	335	256	323	497	531	344

Community and Anti-Social Behaviour

Close-knit kin and neighbourhood structures make it difficult to untangle the complex and dynamic relationships existing within communities, and in particular those that have assumed responsibility for crime management and the development of diversionary projects for young people at risk (Brewer, Lockhart & Rodgers, 1998; Silke & Taylor, 2000; McEvoy & Mika, 2002a). In 1989, Sluka developed the metaphor of paramilitaries as the fish that swim within the water that is their community. The image can still be drawn on to help unpack the notion of a community as an idealised, discretely bounded entity and to see it more dynamically as one in which victims and perpetrators of paramilitary violence share complex and symbiotic relationships. Perhaps the most tangible illustration of this within the public domain is the case of Jonathan Adair, the son of the notorious UDA paramilitary leader, whose "punishment", of being shot through the calves, was sanctioned by his father's closest allies and subalterns.

Fragmenting Family?

The results of the imposition of "informal justice" can have long reaching ramifications, including permanent maiming and psychological scarring that require long-term pharmacological intervention. Yet it is strikingly sad that some young men report that it is preferable to "take the bullet" than to face the exiling that constitutes another significant element in the armoury of social control. Anecdotally, exiling appears to be a less appealing prospect than physical attack.

The pioneering analysis, *The Cost of the Troubles Study* and subsequent articles led by Marie Smyth, remain core reference points for much of the emerging work that grapples with the extent and legacy of the impact of the Troubles on children, young men, and women. Yet, to date, there have been few authors who have identified or alluded to the significance of the impact of exclusion and exiling on children and young people as a result of the conflict (Burrows & Keenan, 2004, p.123; Healey, 2004). Indeed, one of the few pieces of work that looks at those who are exiled to England calls for further work to address this deficit. There is, however, an understandable reluctance on the part of victims and perpetrators to take part in research that they perceive could be used for political ends. Even when work is commissioned and conducted by independent organisations, there is no guarantee that the material will be put in the public domain, because of similar concerns by the commissioning agents (Byrne, 2004).

While activities like this are the subject of widespread media reportage in Northern Ireland, they are rarely viewed within a human rights context that considers the ramifications for children and their families. The possibility of regarding these actions as instances of child abuse remains one of the most academically under-researched and least debated areas of concern.

Consequently, it may be useful here to take a few moments to consider a number of articles from within the United Nations Convention on the Rights of the Child [UNCRC]. Globally, this is the most widely ratified Human Rights Treaty and highlights potential areas where the rights of young people are systematically being violated. These articles provide us with a framework within which to work, a standard with which to hold government to account, and a benchmark from which to begin work in communities. It is when we consider the individual articles that we can appreciate how both physical and exclusionary punishments can result in violations of rights.

Article	
3	Best interests.
15	To be with friends and join or set up clubs, unless this breaks the rights of others.
18	To be brought up by your parents.
19	To be protected from being hurt or badly treated.
24	To health care.
28	To education.
37	Not to be punished in a cruel or hurtful way.
39	To help if you have been hurt, neglected or badly treated.
40	To help in defending yourself if you are accused of breaking the law.

In Northern Ireland, there are many charities, voluntary organisations and children's rights lobbyists who are in a position to explore the issues surrounding paramilitary punishments and the removal of young people from their families and communities. They can employ a child rights-based framework to do this. It is within their remit to work with adults to ensure that they fulfil their obligations to children at risk of these issues, and they can do so at two levels. First, this can be achieved through the communities in which they work, by persuading adults to provide protection to their most vulnerable, marginalised and socially excluded residents. Secondly, they are in a position to hold the government to account for the lack of statutory provision available to those children and young people forced to leave their homes or being punished in a cruel or hurtful way.

However, taking on these roles in a proactive way presents challenges. The first of these comes in terms of teasing out the position between sometimes opposing moral and ethical responsibilities that, in a highly politicised society which is deeply suspicious of the unknown, need to be highlighted to community partners. The second is in urging of the state to fulfil its legal obligations through the development and implementation of sound public policies. For this purpose the Articles of the UNCRC provides us with specific targets, as can be seen on p. 141.

Nevertheless, we are faced with the practicalities of conducting this work in an environment in which we believe that *many young people are exposed to the normalisation of organised violence* and in a *culture where anti-social behaviour has presented itself as a means of resistance.* Transgressing the social norms provides one of the few "weapons of the weak" available to young people who are marginalised and at risk.

Paramilitary youth and Hoods

We need to unpack the above statements a little more, in relation to Northern Ireland having a normalised culture of violence. This can, in part, be attributed to the states' armies and police services, which have provided intentional and unintentional militarised models, both to young people and to paramilitary organisations.

Woolly Faces

The reach of these models is reflected in the use of language, militaristic symbols, iconography and the practice of drilling and parading, and in the use of weapons to both train and to carry out ritualised militaristic funerals (Brett & Specht, 2004). In addition, further connections between these modes of operation can be anecdotally traced to the workings of the growing violent and organised crime networks that influence the areas of piracy, sexual exploitation, and drug racketeering, in all of which young people are active operators.

In relation to Northern Ireland having a culture in which anti-social behaviour is perceived to be growing, it may be useful to consider Nagle's suggestion (2004, p. 10), that for many years a significant minority of young men were "a reservoir of testosterone to be turned off and on like a tap". He draws on popular polar positions, by which some perceive their petty criminality to be drawn on by state forces in order to coerce them into positions of low-level informants. The polar opposite of this is the claim that they were called on by paramilitaries to take part in acts of deviance to disrupt the resources and machinery of the state. Whatever the preferred Machiavellian take on the reasoning behind youth inculcation into anti-social behaviour, there is clearly a visible proportion of young people who perceived themselves, and are perceived by society at large, to fall into the category commonly referred to as *Hoods*. So who are the *Hoods* and what is their relationship to the *Paramilitaries*?

When looking at youth association patterns in working class areas, it is perhaps easiest to draw on and contribute to the early sub-cultural theories of Hall and Jefferson (1976) and Hebdige (1991) to examine the paramilitaries and the Hoods as a sub-class of folk devils.

In some working-class estates of Northern Ireland, young males have a limited choice when aspiring to membership of dominant groups in their areas. They are often restricted to joining or associating with paramilitary organisations. They demonstrate allegiance after initiation by, for example, choices made in peers and friends, in clothing, jewellery, choices of drinking and social venues, and in the marching bands they follow or play in. For some, a paramilitary group provides membership of a principled peer group routed in an ideological framework, which brings with it a set of prescriptive and rigorously cohesive binding mechanisms. As one young combatant said, "When you join, you join for life" (Brett & Specht, 2004, p. 79).

The self-ascribed respectability and pride taken by some of those who chose to join young paramilitary organisations marks them off as members of a separatist and self-appointed policing and governing coalition. As a consequence, their relationship with the statutory police service is *de facto* drawn into question. They become the arbiters of what is acceptable and unacceptable behaviour within the communities that they gate-keep. One young militant explained that, as members of the paramilitary organisation, they use pernicious ways to discourage people from joining or dealing with police officers. "They spray registrations of vehicles on the walls in XXX. Now and then they would do your ma or da and put them out" (Hamilton, Radford & Jarman, 2003, p. 49). The expression, "to do", means in this instance to beat someone up and remove them from the community. This quotation is included to show that paramilitary exiling is both a widespread and well-understood phenomenon within some working-class areas and one that is not directed exclusively at young people. This point will be returned to later, but first it is necessary to consider further the category of Hoods.

The upshot for many who eschew, or who are marginalised from, paramilitary youth sets is being described as a Hood. Hoods, it is no exaggeration to state, are usually the most marginal, most despised members of their communities. Hoods are seen as instigators, or potential instigators, of anti-social behaviour. As such, they are demonised and disempowered by the power imbalances within the communities in which they live. As a consequence of this, they are frequently marginalised from their communities of origin. The subsequent social isolation requires Hoods to develop a particular "street" sense of self-reliance.

"Hooding" brings with it its own markers of membership, in the form of dress codes, patterns of recreational drug use and perceived associations with anti-social behaviour, that feeds into their reputation as disreputable, pro-active criminals. This all courts a constant reactive and proactive conflict with the paramilitaries.

In Northern Ireland, areas are territorialised and marked out in sectarian terms by the flying of national flags and the painting of kerbstones: red, white and blue to denote Loyalist areas and green, white and gold to denote Nationalist areas. Also, paramilitary groups demarcate their "ownership" by the use of paramilitarised murals. As they are devoid of either the will or resources to develop any specific iconographic or iconoclastic markers, the Hoods challenge to authority is the simple graffiti, "UTH" ["Up the Hoods"].

The community gate-keepers respond accordingly, in the form of either statutory or informal policing. "Hoods Beware" was a warning graffiti found in the New Lodge area of Belfast. It demonstrated a direct challenge to the Hoods in an area in which the most established restorative justice programmes in Northern Ireland provide an alternative to statutory policing.

So what are the Hoods to beware of? One method of exerting social, economic and spatial control over areas, and over those who reside and work in them, is through the practice of punishing anyone who persistently violates the social norms and community-espoused codes of conduct. This can include activities such as: noise pollution; harassment; vandalism; burglary; theft; drug dealing; joyriding; and breaching community norms

Those who do so are subject to a variety of punishments, which include: threats; beatings; shootings; and exilings. Exilings, crucifixions, and joint-shattering beatings were at one time *de rigeur* as a form of social control and, while less high profile in media reporting, still occur in many sink estates. When the threat of exiling is directed at whole families, there are wide-sweeping consequences for a variety of age ranges, from siblings and other offspring through to the wider extended family, in which carers might be crucial for keeping those living with disabilities within the community.

"And Stay Out!"

The effects of exiling can include:

A lack of contact with friends.	**cf. Article 15**
Removal from parents.	**cf. Article 18**
Disruption to health care provision.	**cf. Article 24**
Disruption to education.	**cf. Article 28**

It is pertinent at this stage to note that very similar difficulties face those young people who are also forced to move because they have received one of the government's Anti-Social Behaviour Orders. The introduction of the ASBOs in August 2004 in Northern Ireland has been widely condemned by the children's sector, in particular by Save the Children.

Once individuals are exiled to an alien space, their pool of material and cognitive resources are reduced. Young people may have existed within a particularly narrow geographical frame of reference, and they have often had a series of chaotic life experiences, exacerbated by the Troubles. As such, it is perhaps not surprising to find that, in their new and often temporary environment, they frequently lack the motivation and capacity to reconnect with basic services. Further, a sense of social isolation is perpetuated by their weakening ties with family and friends.

I didn't do anything for days. Weeks. I just sat in the flat. I didn't know anybody nor nothing. I had nowhere to go, I was too scared even to go into a bar. I was waking up every time I heard a noise and the child was wetting herself every night because she missed the wee things like one of the teddies we hadn't got with us. But I couldn't even face getting myself a new doctor.

See, after my dad was shot, my ma moved out and I was left with my granny. Then when I was put out for dealing blow, I just stopped going into school, so they threw me out too and so now I just don't bother with school or any of it.

The difficulties that face these young people are exacerbated by the lack of public willingness to address their needs. The provision of services comes with ad hoc arrangements. Whilst it is recognised by all that the needs of the individual children are paramount, social workers fear that, as each case is different, there are no public policies capable of addressing or responding to the broader need. This is certainly reflected by the DHSSPS and the Department of Education, which have no specific policies in place to support those experiencing exiling.

The absence of any clear guidelines is of concern, given that is now several years since the signing of the Good Friday Belfast Agreement (10th April 1998) which incorporated a clear and specific commitment to providing services that are supportive and sensitive to the needs of victims of violence.

Whatever the reason for removal from the community of origin, the needs and rights of young men and women, and of their children and siblings, are often subordinated in their struggle to survive in a new environment. It is pertinent to note that the routes available to them proactively to defend or present their points of view are severely restricted when facing either the brutal legalised justice of ASBOs or the brutal kangaroo court justice of the paramilitaries:

To help in defending yourself if you are accused of breaking the law.	Cf. Article 40

At one level, the restorative justice projects are seen by some young people as addressing the deficit within communities.

> It stops you from having beatings and all, because if you're going to get a beating by the paramilitaries, they would go to them and say, "let us have time with the wee fella", and more or less it stops you getting beating or getting back home.

However, other young people report a degree of scepticism about the process.

> We're just stuck in the middle, so we are. They're just all the same evil scumbags, but now they're dressed up in suits. I hope they get shot in the leg. *(Friend laughs).* No, they do, they do need shot, but….

Conclusion

The focus of this paper has been the practice of paramilitary punishment and exiling, within the context of a debate about the excommunication of children and young people from their communities of origin, alongside the state's lack of support and provision of services to those affected. These violations of children's rights appear to be the elephant in the kitchen, often seen but rarely mentioned, for fear that breaking the silence will upset the fragile checks and balances regulating public discourse and disclosure in a highly politicised society.

By ignoring the issue and avoiding taking and apportioning responsibilities for its perpetuation, individuals, as members of families, communities and workforces, are all in danger of colluding with and condoning these abuses by their silence. By disregarding the veneer of normality that puts a gloss on the symbiotic co-dependent relationships between the community and its gate-keepers, the elected and their electorate can in turn perpetuate the violation of children's rights. With no overarching policy for those young people and their families who have been subject to paramilitary punishments or paramilitary exiling, or who have left their neighbourhoods as a result of ASBOs, it is clear that the *ad hoc* arrangements put in place by statutory service providers are currently missing their mark. Whilst each case presents unique challenges, the best interests of the child are not being met.

Community, peer and family involvement play a crucial role in the social spheres in which young people develop, and may well be core elements in young people's behavioural and decision-making choices. Equally, life-choices are influenced by the displacement and break up of families and poor socio-economic circumstances, including a lack of access to education and employment. Clearly, much of this can be traced back to the legacy of the political conflict and the acceptance of a culture of violence in its many forms.

Appendix

Definitions:

Paramilitary: A contested term, but one taken here to refer to members of organisations, such as (but not exclusively), the Ulster Defence Association [UDA], the Ulster Volunteer Force, [UVF] the Ulster Freedom Fighters [UFF], the Irish Republican Army [IRA], who were known to use physical force and murder against both their enemies and random civilian targets.

Hood: Stereotypically, a young, male, anti-authoritarian figure, with a reputation for engaging in anti-social behaviour.

Punishment Beatings: The use of force by vigilantes or paramilitaries against individuals who offend against their social norms.

Exiling: The temporary or permanent removal by vigilantes or paramilitaries of individuals from their families and communities of origin.

Restorative Justice: Dispute-solving community initiatives informed by United States and New Zealand mediation models. Problems facing the success of such programmes include:

1. The failure of the wider community to claim ownership of the programmes, by recognising their legitimacy;

2. The difficulties associated with the acceptability of policing in some communities and the reluctance of these communities to have statutory involvement within their management.

References

Anderson, D. (1994). *Fourteen May days: The inside story of the Loyalist strike of 1974.* Dublin: Gill and Macmillan.

Base 2 Annual Statistics (2002). Belfast: Niacro.

Beresford, D. (1987). *Ten men dead: The story of the 1981 Irish hunger strike.* London: Grafton.

Boulton, D. (1973). *The UVF, 1966-73. An anatomy of Loyalist rebellion.* Dublin: Gill and Macmillan.

Boyd, A. (1987). *Holy war in Belfast* (3rd ed.). Belfast: Pretani Press. (Original ed. published 1969).

Brett, R., & Specht, I. (2004). *Young soldiers: Why they choose to fight.* London: Lynne Rienner.

Brewer, J. D., Lockhart, B., & Rodgers P. (1998). Informal social control and crime management in Belfast. *British Journal of Sociology*, 49 (4), 570-85.

Bruce, S. (1992). *The red hand: Protestant paramilitaries in Northern Ireland.* Oxford: Oxford University Press.

Burrows, R., & Keenan, B. (2004). Bearing witness: Supporting parents and children in the transition to peace. *Child Care in Practice, 10* (2), 107-25.

Byrne, J. (2004). *Out of sight: Young people and paramilitary exiling in Northern Ireland.* Belfast: Institute for Conflict Research.

Byrne, J., & Monaghan, L. (2009). *Policing Loyalist and Republican communities: Understanding key issues for local communities and the PSNI.* Belfast: Institute for Conflict Research.

Chamberlain, S. (2001). A personal view on the impact of conflict on children and young people. In J. Magowan & N. Patterson (Eds.), *Hear and now .... and then ... : Developments in victims and survivors work.* Belfast: Northern Ireland Voluntary Trust.

Connolly, J. (1997). *Beyond the politics of 'law and order': towards community policing in Ireland.* Belfast: Centre for Research and Documentation.

Conway, P. (1997). Critical reflections: A response to paramilitary policing in Northern Ireland. *Critical Criminology, 8* (2), 109-21.

Coogan, T. P. (1980). *On the blanket: The H Block story.* Dublin: Ward River Press.

Crawford, C. (1999). *Defenders or criminals?: Loyalist prisoners and criminalisation.* Belfast: Blackstaff Press.

Criminal Justice Review Group. (2000). *Review of the criminal justice system in Northern Ireland.* Belfast: Stationery Office.

Dillon, M. (1989) *The Shankill butchers: A case study of mass murder.* London: Hutchinson.

Feenan, D. (2002). Community justice in conflict: Paramilitary punishment in Northern Ireland. In D. Feenan (Ed.), *Informal criminal justice.* Aldershot: Ashgate.

Hall, S., & Jefferson, T. (1976). (Eds.). *Resistance through rituals: Youth subcultures in post-war Britain* (New ed.). London: Hutchinson. (Original ed. published 1975).

Hamilton, J., Radford, K., & Jarman, N. (2003). *Policing, accountability and young people.* Belfast: Institute for Conflict Research.

Healey, A. (2004). A different description of trauma: A wider systemic perspective: A personal insight. *Child Care in Practice, 10* (2), 167-84.

Hebdige, D. (1991). *Subculture: The meaning of style.* London: Routledge.

Jarman, N. (2006). Peacebuilding and policing: the role of community-based initiatives. *Shared Space, 3,* 31-44.

Kennedy, L. (2001). *They shoot children don't they: An analysis of the age and gender of victims of paramilitary "punishments" in Northern Ireland.* Belfast: Queen's University.

Knox, C. (2001). The 'deserving' victims of political violence: 'Punishment' attacks in Northern Ireland. *Criminal Justice, 1* (2), 181-99.

Knox, C., & Monaghan, R. (2002). *Informal justice in divided societies : Northern Ireland and South Africa.* Basingstoke: Palgrave.

McEvoy, K, & Mika, H. (2002b). Republican hegemony or community ownership? Community restorative justice in Northern Ireland. In D. Feenan (Ed.), *Informal criminal justice.* Aldershot: Ashgate.

McEvoy, K., & Mika, H. (2002a). Restorative justice and the critique of informalism in Northern Ireland. *The British Journal of Criminology, 42* (3), 534-62.

McKittrick, D., Kelters, S., Feeney, B., & Thornton, C. (1999). *Lost Lives: The stories of the men, women, and children who died as a result of the Northern Ireland troubles.* Edinburgh: Mainstream.

Monaghan, R. (2002). The return of "Captain Moonlight": Informal justice in Northern Ireland. *Studies in Conflict and Terrorism,* 25 (1), 41-56.

Nagle, J. (2004). *'Up the Hoods': The discursive formation of Belfast youth as Frankenstein's monster, urban guerrilla and folk devil.* Unpublished manuscript, Queen's University, Belfast, Institute of Governance.

Nelson, S. (1984). *Ulster's uncertain defenders: Protestant political, paramilitary and community groups and the Northern Ireland conflict.* Belfast: Appletree Press.

Radford, K., Hamilton, J., & Jarman, N. (2005) 'It's their word against mine': Young people's attitudes to the police complaints procedure in Northern Ireland. *Children & Society,* 19 (5), 360-70.

Shirlow, P., & McGovern, M. (Eds.). (1997). *Who are 'the people'?: Unionism, Protestantism and Loyalism in Northern Ireland.* London: Pluto Press.

Silke, A., & Taylor, M. (2000). War without end: Comparing IRA and Loyalist vigiliantism in Northern Ireland. *The Howard Journal of Criminal Justice,* 39 (3), 249-66.

Smyth, M. (Proj. Dir.). (1999). *Final report: The Cost of the Troubles Study.* Belfast: Cost of the Troubles Study Ltd.

Sluka, J. A. (1989). *Hearts and minds, water and fish: Support for the IRA and INLA in a Northern Irish ghetto.* Greenwich, CT: JAI Press.

United Nations Convention on the Rights of the Child (1992). Retrieved 26 January 2010: http://www2.ohchr.org/english/law/crc.htm

Winston, T. (1997). Alternatives to punishment beatings and shootings in a Loyalist community in Belfast. *Critical Criminology,* 8 (1), 122-8.

"PRISON WITHOUT BARS": THE IMPACT OF IMPRISONMENT ON FAMILIES

Nancy Loucks

When people think about "Fragmenting Families", imprisonment is unlikely to be the first issue that springs to their mind. Indeed, this is generally a much neglected area of research. This paper shows how relevant a topic imprisonment is and, in view of tougher sentencing policies and the subsequent increase in the use of imprisonment, how important it is to consider the impact on families. The paper begins with the general impact imprisonment has on families, the benefits of maintaining family ties and the key pressure points. These sections are largely based on a review of information available internationally (Loucks, 2004a). The next section discusses feedback from prisoners' families taken from specially commissioned pieces of work including: the Tayside Family Project (Loucks, 2004b); research into prison visitors' centres (Loucks 2002); research into young parents in prison (Sherlock, 2004; Loucks, 2005); and research into the role of family contact workers in prisons (Loucks, 2005). This is followed by an outline of existing resources for families, including gaps in provision. The paper ends with an overview of the type of provision which would seem to be helpful in supporting families and in assisting them in maintaining family ties, should they wish to do so.

The impact of imprisonment on family ties

Imprisonment is a family experience. Every year in England and Wales, an estimated 150,000 children are separated from a parent by imprisonment, with up to 17,700 separated from an imprisoned mother (Prison

Reform Trust, 2005). People under the age of 21 are held an average of 51 miles or more from their home area, while nearly a fifth of female prisoners are held over 100 miles away from their committal court town. Such distances make visits to imprisoned family members extremely difficult. Entering prisons can also be very intimidating. As a result of such strains, the Social Exclusion Unit in England and Wales (2002; also the National Association for the Care and Resettlement of Offenders, 2000) found that 43% of sentenced prisoners and 48% of remand prisoners lost contact with their families when they entered prison. Her Majesty's Chief Inspector of Prisons (2001) also found that only about half of prisoners use their minimum entitlement to visits.

Basically, imprisonment radically alters the family dynamic. This is the case even when prisoners are in relatively close contact with their families, such as when they are in open establishments. A prisoner who had spent the last three years in an open prison in England noted:

> ... my marriage survived the sentence, but not the release. When I returned home it soon became evident that things had changed. Instead of my wife and children relying on me for everything, they had become independent, self-sufficient. They had learnt to live without me. I felt surplus to needs.... Perhaps we should concentrate more on the emotional challenges of release, and not just the material things. (Seward, 2002, p. 24)

In his report into a series of disturbances at a number of prisons in 1990, Lord Justice Woolf commented:

> The disruption of the inmate's position within the family unit represents one of the most distressing aspects of imprisonment.... Enabling inmates, so far as possible, to stay in close and meaningful contact with the family is therefore an essential part of humane treatment.... There is every reason to believe that the nature of a prisoner's relationship with his or her family will be an important factor in determining whether he or she will succeed in leading a

useful and law-abiding life on return to the community. (Woolf & Tumim, 1991, chap. 14, para. 223)

Woolf described this disruption as one of the most difficult consequences of incarceration and encouraged intervention to minimise such disruption.

For prisoners, separation from their family can be the most painful consequence of incarceration. The literature, national and international, shows a dramatic affect of imprisonment on families (Loucks, 2004a). This is not to minimise the experiences of victims of crime, but rather to understand that victimisation can be indirect as well as direct. Families have often been described as the "forgotten victims" of crime. Families suffer the pain of separation, but also feel the impact of imprisonment in other ways, such as:

> • Loss of income – often the main wage-earner is the one in custody. Benefits may be reduced, or the family may be left responsible to pay for debts or compensation;
> • Loss of home – a reduction in income may mean they cannot afford to stay where they are, or they may be targeted by neighbours or people connected with any victims;
> • Anti-social behaviour by children in distress - this is discussed briefly below;
> • Shame - shame is an important category, as it often prevents families from seeking out the help they need or indeed from taking advantage of support that may be offered to them;
> • Transport - the cost and logistics of transport can be a formidable barrier to contact. Families Outside (2003) found that almost half of prisoners' families in Scotland spend between five and twelve hours making a return journey on a prison visit. Visiting

times may also be inconvenient for families who work, or have children in school.

Impact on children

Children of prisoners are at higher risk of imprisonment in later life. Research in California noted that children of incarcerated parents are five to six times more likely to go to prison than their peers (Gabel & Johnston, 1995). Physical symptoms, mental health problems, and regressive behaviour, such as bed-wetting, can also begin with the incarceration of a parent or other family member. Children of female prisoners are likely to face the additional disruption of multiple care arrangements during their mother's imprisonment. The Prison Reform Trust (2005) note that only 5% of the children of female prisoners remain in their own home once their mother has been sentenced. Many parents choose not to tell children about the imprisonment of a family member. However, the children often realise it themselves, or hear about the imprisonment from another source, before they have the opportunity to understand about it or to ask questions. A review of young parents in prison (Sherlock, 2004) looked at provision for parents up to the age of 25, who were therefore more likely to have younger children. The report showed particular problems for younger children, who do not understand why Mum or Dad cannot get up and play with them, or why they cannot come home with them or even leave the prison for a short time. Communication by telephone or letter is very difficult with this age group. This adds to distress for parents and carers and makes the quality of prison visits even more important.

In sum, the family takes on the characteristics of a single parent family. This includes a greater likelihood of experiencing poverty, unemployment, isolation, and deterioration in physical and mental health. These stresses, plus the stress of separation itself, mean that relations between partners often break down when one of them is in custody. In effectively living the life of a single parent and spending all of their free time in travel and visits to prison, partners of prisoners have described their own lives as "living in a prison without bars" (Christensen, 2001, p. 85).

Benefits of maintaining family ties

In view of the statistics, improving contact between prisoners and their families is surely a noble goal. However, assisting prisoners and their families in this way has greater benefits than just "being nice". We know, for example, that family breakdown is a risk factor for suicides in custody (Akhurst, Brown & Wessely, 1995). We also know from research in the United States that maintaining family ties decreases the risk of reoffending by six times (Holt & Miller, 1972; Ditchfield, 1994). These findings are also easily explained. Better ties with people outside means a better chance of housing, employment, and general social support, all of which relate to the risk of offending.

Research has also shown benefits in terms of decreased reoffending, improved mental health for prisoners and their families, and an increased likelihood of families reuniting after release (Hairston, 1991). The Scottish Forum on Prisons and Families and the Scottish Prison Service (2000) found that prison halls were easier to manage when prisoners were better able to maintain contact with their families. Prisoners were more content when they had good quality contact with their families and when they and their families had the support to help them to achieve this.

A report for the Prison Reform Trust (Loucks, 2005) noted that families themselves need support for a number of reasons. Visitors are often unaware of their entitlements or are very hesitant to ensure that these are respected (see Neto & Wilson, 1982). Visitors do not "demand" a service and may fear repercussions for their loved one in prison if they ask for information or support. However, lack of demand does not equate to lack of need. Prisoners themselves often do not have a clear understanding of their family's needs during their imprisonment. Furthermore, research in the USA found that services developed for offenders, their children and families, to support them and to enhance their integration into the community, show particular promise in reducing reoffending (Johnson, Selber & Lauderdale, 1998). Overall, support for families and prisoners in maintaining contact has a number of potential benefits, both in terms of increased humanity and in the more tangible terms of reduced offending and improved health and well-being for all parties.

Key pressure points

The whole experience of imprisonment places tremendous strain on prisoners' families. One question is whether particular periods are more difficult than others.

> • *The initial arrest.* Imprisonment, even when arrest is anticipated, is usually a sudden event. Much of the damage is caused by the arrest and imprisonment itself, regardless of the length of time a prisoner spends in custody. Before imprisonment, families are not likely to have had an opportunity to discuss issues such as childcare, housing or income with the prisoner. If the primary carer is taken into custody, urgent arrangements must be made for childcare. For children and young people, the period immediately following the arrest is the worst period, not least because of the sudden change of

circumstances, a sense of powerlessness, lack of information and possible uncertainty in relation to care arrangements.

• *Prison visits.* Lack of information about visits and visiting procedures, inconvenient visiting times and booking systems, perceptions of staff attitudes, the prison environment and drug detection procedures all act as disincentives to prison visits. Children show signs of stress both before and after visits, including sickness, irritability, excessive quietness or over-excitement prior to visits, restlessness and argumentative behaviour during visits, and sadness or withdrawn behaviour afterwards. Visits bring a range of both positive and negative emotions. Children get bored during visits, which both prisoners and carers have identified as one of the most difficult aspects of prison visiting.

• *Preparation for release.* Families are rarely included in a prisoner's preparation for release from custody, despite the fact that it can be a particularly stressful and frightening period for them. The likelihood of difficulty in finding employment, financial problems, learning to live together again as a couple, sexual anxieties and worries about relationships with children all highlight the need for support for prisoners and their families at the pre-release stage, especially for sentenced prisoners.

• *After release.* The difficulties in adjustment after release often come as a surprise to families, especially after a long sentence. Partners will (hopefully) have learned to cope independently, and children will have grown and may have few memories of life with the other parent in the house.

• *Throughout custody.* Essentially, the entire period of custody presents difficulties, some of which will be more difficult than others, depending on individual circumstances. A partner of a long-term prisoner said that the worst part for her was the middle of the sentence:

> At the beginning you have so many things going on, you just have to get on with it. Once things have settled, you really begin to feel lost.... It's difficult to describe.... You know the end is in sight, but it might still be a long while off. You're stuck between the two; everything gets you down, weighs upon you. And just before release – though this passes more quickly because you're so wound up about the release – getting things ready at home. (Loucks, 2004b)

The overall picture is that most families need material assistance, support, and advice throughout the period of imprisonment, regardless of its duration.

Feedback from families

A number of reports have looked at the impact of imprisonment on families by canvassing their views. The Tayside Family Project (Loucks, 2004b) reported responses from 50 families, 13 of which were followed up in more depth with telephone interviews, and a further six with a group discussion. The Prison Reform Trust's Young Parents' Project, reported in Sherlock (2004) and Loucks (2005), followed young parents, their families, and the staff who work with them, over a period of a year in England, Scotland and Northern Ireland. Further work by the Prison Reform Trust looked at the role of family contact officers in prisons in the UK (Loucks, 2005). Earlier research conducted on behalf of the Prison Reform Trust and Action for Prisoners' Families examined the role of prison visitors' centres (Loucks, 2002). The findings reported below represent a combination of the responses families gave during all of these projects.

"Prison Without Bars"

The research projects asked a number of questions about family members' own experiences and that of their families. In general, the most damage to families following imprisonment appears to be to their emotional health. About two-thirds believed that the emotional well-being of themselves and their family had worsened. Expressions of family members' own sense of imprisonment were not uncommon, with comments such as "… you feel like you're in gaol yourself", or "I feel *I'm* paying the price for his mistake" being prominent amongst their replies.

Many people believed that they had suffered financially because of the imprisonment (59% for themselves, and 45% for other family members).   Significant numbers also reported being worse off in terms of their physical health and safety, social and family life, state benefits and family support.   The relationship with the person they were visiting was a particular concern with regard to others in the family (41%), although, interestingly, many people believed that their own relationship with the imprisoned person had improved (23%).

Comments from family members included: "[I have had] no support from [the family] as they think I should just have walked away. I understand this, but feel a bit let down, as I have been there for them when they had bad times in their lives."   A partner of a prisoner said: "My family and friends don't agree with me standing by my partner, therefore I don't have any support." The wife of one prisoner added: "I don't feel that I get enough time to spend with my partner as I would like. I think it would be a good idea if he had less visits but more time on one visit, as I cannot afford to travel all the time, and he can't afford to phone me a lot." Parents of prisoners also suffered: "My son is full of good ideas and intentions when he phones me from prison, but when he is home for the weekend visits all his good intentions go out the window. It can be stressful."

Imprisonment could have very severe consequences for families. This is evident in the response from one man, who said: "My family has been torn apart, my wife and I have separated, my daughter and her family's relationship with myself is very strained and her relationship with her mother is over."

On top of the personal crises, a number of families were under threat from victims or the victim's friends and family. This could mean changes in their daily routine, including changing the places where they shopped, loss of business as the publicity from the case spread, or even the need to move away from the area. In the case of one woman, both herself and her two-year old daughter were threatened on the street and had stab-marks left in their door. It took the council 18 months to move her elsewhere.

Threats of this kind must be taken seriously. The murder in England of Joan and John Stirland, reported in the media in August 2004, is a case in point. The murder is a tragic story in itself, but it is particularly notable in the current context because they were targeted as a consequence of Mrs Stirland's son being in prison for murder. Her *son* was in prison, yet she and her husband had to go into hiding and were eventually tracked down and became the victims of a revenge attack.

The Tayside Project (Loucks, 2004b) asked respondents to say what they believed were the most difficult aspects of imprisonment for themselves and their families. In order of frequency, these included:

- Worry about the prisoner (87.5%);
- Separation from the prisoner (77.1%);
- Worry about what will happen after release (60.4%);
- Cost of travel for visits (56.3%);
- Lack of information (43.8%);

- Lack of support (39.6%);
- What to tell others (37.5%);
- Transportation to the prison (37.5%);
- Timing of visits (37.5%);
- Financial problems (33.3%);
- Worry about the family (22.9%);
- Housing (22.9%);
- Media attention (18.8%);
- Loss of friends (16.7%);
- Employment (6.3%).

Families clearly experience a number of difficulties, but the majority of responses suggest that the direct impact of imprisonment, namely separation from a loved one and barriers to contact with that person, is the most trying for them.

A minority response, but an important one nonetheless, was from the families who felt they were better off during the prisoner's incarceration. Contrary to reporting that imprisonment had put a strain on their lives, one parent had said that it was "a holiday" to be relieved from regular threats and violence from their heroin-addicted son. One or two other families had also been subject to constant manipulation or financial demands, usually to feed addictions, from family members now in custody. Concerns about release in such cases were not restricted to the prisoner's welfare, but were about their own financial stability and even their physical safety.

Support upon release was a general concern for all families. One mother believed that her son would not have been recalled to prison had adequate support been in place. A number of families expressed general disillusionment about the opportunities for prisoner rehabilitation available, both inside and after release. Respondents were looking for support in a number of areas:

- Preparation for release (63.6%);
- Information about parole/non-parole licences (59.1%);
- Information about what organisations can do for ex-prisoners (59.1%);
- More information about the prisoner (54.5%);
- Advice about how to keep the prisoner out of trouble in the future (50.0%);
- Better quality of contact (47.7%);
- Information about what help social work staff can offer ex-prisoners (47.7%);
- More contact with the person inside (43.2%);
- More information about the prison (40.9%);
- Someone to talk to (34.1%);
- Financial help and advice (31.8%);
- More support for children (25.0%);
- Help with childcare (11.4%);
- Advice on what to tell others (9.1%);
- Housing (9.1%).

Clearly, families would appreciate assistance on a wide range of issues. Better provision of information, particularly with regard to release and the preparation for this, stood out as a priority. Family contact, especially good quality contact, was also a prominent request.

The need for support could often be quite basic. Comments included: "Just having someone to talk to about how I feel"; "Friends to speak to"; and "Talking about experiences, sharing attitudes, etc". "People that have been through the same as you" appeared regularly in their responses. Family and friends may be more able to provide the timely support the respondents need: "... friends understood what was happening, but all the other areas we tried for help were too long-winded. We needed the help at the time we asked for it and it wasn't there."

By far the most common avenues of support were family (69.0%) and friends (59.5%). Other resources, such as visitors' centres, were used when these were available, but often families became frustrated with more formal avenues of support. Prison staff, social workers and solicitors came under criticism. Almost none of the families had heard of Families Outside (see below), or of the Scottish Prisoners' Families' Helpline, or of family contact officers. Families did not necessarily sense a lack of support from these groups. It was more the fact that families did not know who to turn to at initial custody, during imprisonment, and in preparation for release. The quest for information seemed to them to be a constant battle. One family member commented that families were "just left completely in the dark... [it's] always 'pass the buck, pass the buck', put on to someone else ... just like a vicious circle ... like nobody cares." Another said that she "felt like [she] was banging [her] head off a brick wall".

Access to information was a crucial issue, but the families agreed that they just needed to know where they could go for information; at which point, they could decide for themselves what they wanted to do.

Existing resources

On a more positive note, a number of resources are available for families. In Scotland, Families Outside is the only organisation that works exclusively on behalf of children, parents, spouses, partners and other family members of people in custody. In England and Wales, Action for Prisoners' Families acts as the main umbrella organisation, with a remit similar to that of Families Outside. Other organisations provide designated services for prisoners' families in the UK, as part of a wider remit.

Locally based organisations in England, such as BARS, HALOW and POPS, provide support for families in specific areas or even at specific prisons. Prison services throughout the UK have made substantial progress towards improving family contact in recent years. Play facilities in visit halls, and in visitors' centres where they exist, are a notable improvement (Loucks, 2002). Family days and separate parent/child visits concentrate on improving the quality of visits between parents and children. Even more liberal provision is evident in other countries, including organised private family visits over a 72-hour period in Canada, France and Spain.

Visitors' centres are worth considering in more detail. A visitors' centre is usually a building (permanent or temporary) separate from the prison, usually run by outside organisations, prison staff, or a combination of the two. The quality of these facilities varies widely across the UK. The perceived purpose of the visitors' centre also varies. During the research (Loucks, 2002), the way centre managers described the purpose of their visitors' centre at the beginning of the questionnaire informed us, without fail, what type of organisation ran it, though we did not ask who ran the centre until the end of the questionnaire. Visitors' centres run by private or voluntary sector organisations typically described their purpose in ways such as: " To provide a warm welcome for visitors to [the prison] and friendly support at all times; to provide help with practical difficulties; to provide information, and a listening ear to those in need"; or: "To meet the needs of all visiting relatives or friends in [prison] by providing: a pleasant, safe welcoming environment, dignity, respect, and the opportunity to discuss difficulties and worries; to provide clear, full, and relevant information." Visitors' centres run by the prison, however, tended to follow a different pattern, describing their purpose in different terms, for example: "To provide a muster point for visitors to assemble in the hope that visitors can be processed in a quick and efficient manner."

Feedback from governors of prisons with a good quality visitors' centre was extremely positive: "For the cost of less than one officer, we get contented visitors, leading to good visits, producing contented prisoners"; or: "To give the information/support required to families in a remote geographical area would be almost impossible without the visitors' centre." Families, too, tended to respond positively to the support they received from visitors' centres, especially when other support for families is virtually non-existent.

Family support work in prisons is also worthy of mention, especially as it exists in few prisons outside Scotland (see Loucks, 2005). Family support staff are prison employees or civilian workers with an overall responsibility for families. Generally they are responsible for developing policies to support family contact, for hearing complaints from families about visits or other matters, and ideally for involving families in aspects of the prison regime. Very few family support officers exist in England and Wales, although the posts exist in all of the Scottish prisons. However, their impact varies widely.

Family support staff (family contact and development officers [FCDOs)] in Scotland) provide an important link to families who may otherwise be sidelined. For example, special visits have been arranged, such as a visit outside normal hours, arranged for a child who was severely disabled, so that the visit could "take place with more dignity for the child and prisoner." Special visits and support have also been arranged following the death of family members. In one case, the child of a woman in custody had died. The FCDO arranged for a private visit for the family at the prison after the funeral and away from the regular visiting area, and with facilities to make tea and coffee. They were able to provide support and information for families. FCDOs were able to ease family concerns about bullying and suicides by arranging extra visits for the mother of a boy who had been assaulted in custody. In another prison, FCDOs arranged a special visit for the parent of a 16-year old who had just received a life sentence. The visit included a pre-arranged meeting with her and a tour of the establishment.

FCDOs were also able to assist with family contact. On one occasion, the worker helped a boy to write a letter to his father after the father had put the telephone down on him twice. The FCDO then contacted the father and was able to restore the relationship. FCDOs were also able to encourage joint working with families on issues such as addiction and distress. In one prison, FCDOs and family members worked together to encourage prisoners to "detox" from drugs. European research has found co-operative efforts between prisons, prisoners and families to be very important in the support of families of drug users (Hennebel, Fowler & Costall, 2002).

This type of support may be available in prisons without an FCDO, perhaps through the chaplaincy. The problem is that prisons that lack a specific focus on family work tend to overlook the issue, or to provide support only on an ad hoc basis. Family-focused work has tremendous potential in prisons. HMP Cornton Vale, a prison for women in Scotland, has staff trained in family group counselling, to assist families in dealing with crises that may arise during periods of custody. The prison has also set up a new unit called the St Margaret's Centre, which exists specifically for the prison's work with families.

The potential remit of family support staff in prisons is very broad. While none of the prisons in this research provided all of this support, most provided at least part of it. Provision of information at the point of arrest and in the courts is one important aspect where assistance is required, although very few prisons tackle this. Courts are under no obligation to provide information to families. When someone is sent to prison, families may have no idea where the person is being sent, or how to get there, or how to arrange a visit. Information and assistance for prisoners on remand and their families is another important area, especially as support at the remand stage tends to take lower priority. Information, advice and support during a sentence can include: staff acting as a contact point for prisoners' families; assistance with visits (booking, travel costs, special visits, parent/child visits); crisis support; and links with relevant agencies outside. Some family support staff run parenting courses for prisoners, or manage schemes in which parents in prison can tape-record or video stories for their children. Pre-release courses for prisoners and families can provide vital assistance to prepare for their lives after custody. Information and training for all categories of prison staff is important, to enlighten them about the impact of imprisonment on families and relevant child protection issues. Finally, general outreach work can include awareness sessions for sentencers and contacts with outside agencies for support on issues such as addiction, debt, housing and employment.

A number of initiatives highlight examples of good practice for work with prisoners' families. "Starting Where They Are" is an example of support for adolescents in England. Its aim is to raise awareness of the issue of prisoners' families in schools. Taking advantage of a pre-existing service avoids the stigma of a specific "issue-based" service and preserves the confidentiality of users. Support is based in schools, is flexible and provides one-to-one or group support, depending on the needs of participants (see Brown, 2003; Brown, DeBell, & Andi, 2003).

Another project, the Young People's Support Service at HMP Durham, consists of a separate room within the visitors' centre, specifically for teenage visitors. The room provides age-appropriate activities, with a paid support worker and two volunteers in attendance. The room offers a space for young people to await visits, contact with other young people in a similar situation, age-appropriate information, and "a conduit for one-to-one support with the support worker or for family support" (Brown et al., 2003, p. 7).

One programme in Oregon USA is designed to address needs at the key stages of incarceration. The first step in the programme is to assign an advocate to a child immediately upon a parent's arrest. Upon incarceration, all inmates are needs-assessed and identified as to whether or not they are parents. A team at the prison develops a sentence plan that includes parenting classes for parents. Finally, a parenting component is included in the prisoner's preparations for release (see Loucks, 2004a).

Leaflets and internet sites are becoming increasingly available for prisoners' families and those who work with them. EUROCHIPS is one that pulls together information from organisations all over Europe. Specialised publications, for example on the needs of young people in prison, are increasingly available. One good example is *"Daddy's Working Away"* (Rice & Watson, 2003), a booklet written by prisoners and families at the Wolds Prison in England, and published by Care for the Family in Cardiff.

Gaps in provision

A number of organisations can be useful in the support of prisoners' families. However, their remits do not usually identify prisoners' families specifically as a target group. No single organisation is responsible for the direct co-ordination and provision of services to prisoners' families in the UK. Furthermore, the failure of so many general support services to recognise and plan specifically for prisoners' families seems to be an important oversight.

Few organisations formally acknowledge prisoners' families as a distinct group within the remit of their work. Only after the existence of this (extremely hidden) group is acknowledged and identified can specific work be done to address their needs. Even with family support staff in prisons, a specific "voice" or advocate for children is virtually non-existent. The need for information in courts, prior to imprisonment, is another obvious gap in provision for families. Preparation for release and better linkages with community-based social structures and support services all need further development.

Often the need is not so much to fill gaps as to strengthen the resources already available. This was notable in the Tayside Project (Loucks, 2004b), in which families identified gaps such as:

> • A network of more locally-based support, such as a family support group;
> • More awareness of existing support, such as family contact and development officers, Families Outside, and the Scottish Prisoners' Families Helpline; and
> • More participation in prison-based activities, sentence planning, and resettlement.

What works?

The literature highlights that families can play an important part in helping prisoners through their sentences, and in contributing to sentence management and prison regimes. Prisoners who have family support cope better during imprisonment and are less likely to reoffend upon release than those who do not. What is less clear is what support and intervention is helpful for *families* of people in prison. This type of support is difficult, if not impossible, to measure in quantitative terms. The relative lack of "hard" data does not mean, however, that initiatives in this area are not worthwhile.

Information

The target audiences must be considered carefully, and the information provided should include specific priorities. Resources should also be up-to-date and, ideally, linked to the internet. Finally, access to the information is at least as important as the information itself.

Families should have information about visits provided in advance of their arrival at a prison. Family induction schemes are an ideal opportunity to provide comprehensive information to families and, importantly, to give them an opportunity to ask questions.

Visitors' centres

Good visits are essential to good relations and the maintenance of family ties. Supporting visits through a visitors' centre is a logical way of maintaining a prisoner's family ties, or other links with the outside world. Lack of a prison visitors' centre often creates difficulty for families who do not know where to go for support, and also for organisations trying to access prisoners' families.

Family support staff

Family support work, including that carried out by FCDOs in Scotland, shows great potential for addressing the needs of prisoners' families. The work of family support staff provides abundant evidence of benefits to families, and equally to prison regimes and security.

Programmes and support projects

Support groups are the key to helping families. Support services and programmes in prisons must have the backing of prison managers and staff, although the limited "hard evidence" of the success of these projects means that both staff support and funding can be in short supply. The positive feedback and overwhelming weight of experience from people and organisations that work in this area, however, demonstrates that this work is highly valuable.

Consultation with families

We were very pleased to get feedback from families through the various pieces of research discussed here. Prisoners' families can be a very difficult group to access, but the various projects, and in particular the Tayside Family Project (Loucks, 2004b), show that this is not impossible. Consultation is essential if appropriate services are to be developed.

Conclusions

The imprisonment of a family member clearly has a significant impact on those left outside. Families are unwilling participants in a system they find intimidating, disempowering and utterly frustrating, and in which they may have no experience, no control and no voice. Some may in turn become victims themselves, through circumstances which they cannot control and are no fault of their own.

Many support services have been developed in recent years, and examples of good practice are in evidence nationally and internationally. A number of positive initiatives currently exist to support prisoners' families. However, many schemes depend largely on the initiative and enthusiasm of a few dedicated staff.

Factors such as fear of stigma or lack of knowledge and awareness often prevent families from accessing the supports that exist for them. As a matter of urgency, assistance in the maintenance of family ties and support for prisoners' families should become an integral part of the regime in prisons, as well as an acknowledged remit of organisations outside, if they are to target their work appropriately and effectively.

References

Akhurst, M., Brown, I., & Wessely, S. (1995). *Dying for help: Offenders at risk of suicide.* Wakefield: West Yorkshire Probation Service.

Brown K. (2003). *Young people's support service: Supporting young people with a prisoner in the family.* London: Action for Prisoners' Families.

Brown, K., DeBell, D., & Andi, S. (2003). *Exploring the needs of young people with a prisoner in the family.* London: Action for Prisoners' Families.

Christensen, E. (2001). Imprisoned parents and their families: What can we do to minimise harmful effects to children? *Journal of Child Centred Practice, 8*, 84-5.

Ditchfield, J. (1994). Family ties and recidivism: Main findings of the literature. *Home Office Research Bulletin, 36*, 3-9.

Families Outside. (2003). *A review of services for families accessing Scottish prisons*. Edinburgh: Author.

Gabel, K., & Johnston, D. (Eds.). (1995). *Children of incarcerated parents*. New York: Lexington Books.

Hairston, C. F. (1991). Family ties during imprisonment: Important to whom and for what? *Journal of Sociology and Social Welfare, 18*, 87-104.

Hennebel, L. C., Fowler, V., & Costall, P. (2002). *Supporting families of drug-dependent offenders*. London: European Network of Drug Services in Prison.

Her Majesty's Chief Inspector of Prisons for England and Wales. (2001). *Report, 1999-2000*. London: Stationery Office.

Holt, N., & Miller, D. (1972). *Explorations in inmate-family relationships*. Sacramento: California Department of Corrections Research.

Johnson, T., Selber, K., & Lauderdale, M. (1998). Developing quality services for offenders and families: An innovative partnership. *Child Welfare, 77*, 595-615.

Loucks, N. (2002). *Just visiting?: A review of the role of prison visitors' centres*. London: Prison Reform Trust.

Loucks, N. (2004a). *'Prison without bars': Needs, support, and good practice for work with prisoners' families*. Dundee: Tayside Criminal Justice Partnership; Edinburgh: Families Outside.

Loucks, N. (2004b). *The Tayside Family Project*. Dundee: Tayside Criminal Justice Partnership; Edinburgh: Families Outside.

Loucks, N. (2005). *Keeping in touch: The case for family support work in prisons*. London: Prison Reform Trust.

National Association for the Care and Resettlement of Offenders. (2000). *The forgotten majority: The resettlement of short term prisoners*. London: Author.

Neto, V., & Wilson, D. (1982). *An evaluation of the Centerforce network of visitor centers at California state prisons*. Washington, DC: National Institute of Corrections.

Prison Reform Trust. (2005). [Press release on *Keeping in touch: The case for family support work in prisons*, by N. Loucks]. London: Author.

Rice, S., & Watson, S. (2003). *"Daddy's working away": A guide to being a dad in prison*. Cardiff: Care for the Family.

Scottish Forum on Prisons and Families, & Scottish Prison Service. (2000). *Report on facilities for families visiting prisons in Scotland in 2000: Implementing the standards and increasing good practice: First annual report of the Joint Standing Committee*. Edinburgh: Authors.

Seward, L. (2002). Valuing relationships. *Prison Report, 58,* 22-24.

Sherlock, J. (2004). *Young parents: From custody to community: A guide to policy and practice*. London: Prison Reform Trust.

Social Exclusion Unit. (2002). *Reducing re-offending by ex-prisoners*. London: Author.

Woolf, H., & Tumim, S. (1991). *Prison disturbances April 1990: Report of an inquiry*. London: HMSO.

WHEN TWO BECOME THREE (OR MORE): THE EFFECTS OF PARENTHOOD ON RELATIONSHIPS

Vicki Ford

This paper has as its focus the changes people experience when they decide to become parents and create a family of their own. As Elizabeth Martyn says in her book, *Baby Shock*, "Making the decision to have a child is not like changing jobs or buying a new car. It's a decision that involves two people intimately and has life-long consequences." (2001, p. 17).

That said, having children is one of the most natural events in the human life cycle. For most people, the announcement that a baby is expected is one of life's happiest and most joyous occasions. It is a time for celebration and renewal, as families move up the life cycle hierarchy and children become adults, adults become parents, parents become grandparents. It is, perhaps, reasonable to assume that there is little more to be said about such a normal life event.

Contemporary families are very diverse in relation to their composition and the so-called nuclear family is in decline. Government information on households (Office for National Statistics, 2005) shows that the word "family" no longer just means Mum, Dad and 2.2 children (plus dog!). People live together in many different social groupings. These include parents with adult children, brothers and sisters buying property together, grandparents bringing up grandchildren as their own (sometimes the child is unaware that "Aunty" Pat is actually their mum!), lone parents, gay/lesbian and polyamourous households, stepfamilies, households headed by adoptive parents or foster parents. Others come to view communes or residential units as home.

Despite all of these permutations, a man and a woman living together and having children continues to be recognised by the majority as the norm. Couples are the focus of this paper. However, this is not to dismiss the very real issues that face single mothers, or any other of the family groupings mentioned above.

In my work as a relationship counsellor and psychosexual therapist, I have come across many couples for which the transition to parenthood has been extremely difficult. I wish here to highlight some of the issues couples have presented during counselling and psychosexual therapy. Many of the couples I have seen were totally unprepared for the challenges of a new baby; not only for the work involved, but also for the effect on the couple's relationship. When a couple become parents, their relationship changes irrevocably. No longer can they put themselves first. This new person needs a lot of attention, and this can result in new mothers feeling exhausted and new fathers feeling sidelined. For the majority, this new role is an extremely rewarding experience. For others, it is harder to cope with. Some are overwhelmed by a sense of being taken over, even invaded. This can have a huge impact on couples. In some cases, it can lead to depression, to violence against the children, and to relationship breakdown. This paper draws solely upon the reported experiences of couples that have sought help. However, it is reasonable to assume that there are many more couples who suffer in silence, unable to admit that they are finding parenthood a strain:

> Having a baby can be one of the most rewarding experiences any couple can have. The miracle of a new life, and the fact that you have created it, can bring a couple closer together than any other life event. Unfortunately, the opposite can also be true, and in these

cases, rather than being a blessing, the baby can create tension and unhappiness. (Ford, 2005, p. 49)

The role of the father during the first few months after the baby is born is very important. He needs to be both patient and supportive. This can be hard when feelings of rejection, and competition for attention and for affection, take over. A delicate balancing act between the couple is played out. Winnicott coined the phrase "good enough mother" (1971). Here, the use of this term is extended to "good enough couple". If they can be supportive of each other, have a sense of what the other is experiencing, and can express this, emotionally, physically and psychologically, they can adapt to their new roles well. If the scales tip over onto one side, the other partner can feel left out and isolated. New mums often receive a lot of attention if they have family and friends to support them. In contrast, new dads can often get pushed out. This happened to John. He and his wife had waited a long time for their baby and, when she finally arrived, he felt as if he had lost his wife, as she was so completely wrapped up in the baby, and the praise she got from everyone made it feel as if he did not exist.

Where there is no outside support, pressure is put on Dad to be all things. Fiona had her baby in a town hundreds of miles away from her family and friends. She suffered with post-natal depression and relied heavily on her husband when he came home from a very demanding job. As he could not cope, he too eventually became depressed. Fortunately, her health visitor was alerted to the problem and referred them to counselling. She was also on hand to help them to adjust to their new life. Occasionally, new fathers can be so caught up with this little person that Mum scarcely gets a look in. Jealously is a very difficult emotion to own up to, especially when it is manifested towards your own child. Sue had felt that she ceased to exist in her husband's eyes once her baby was born.

The quality of the relationship *before* and *during* pregnancy can impact on how things may develop after the birth. Marc Ganem, a consultant gynaecologist from Paris, has carried out some very interesting research relating to sex and pregnancy, following 600 couples over a ten-year period. He discovered that those couples who were sexually intimate up to and including the eighth month of pregnancy were less likely to experience sexual difficulties after the birth. He also found that there was:

- Less likelihood of "baby blues";
- Less likelihood of depression;
- Easier initiation of sexual intercourse;
- Shorter time before making love again;
- Better communication between the couple regarding the nurturing of the baby. (Ganem, 2004)

As a nation, we are not good at talking about sex in general. Discussion between the couple regarding the quality of their sex life when the woman is pregnant is likely to prove to be even more problematic.

Some men do not realise the impact of their behaviour on their wives/partners during pregnancy. For example, one client was faced with a partner who could not bear to see her body "distorted" in such a "grotesque" way (as he put it). Even more damagingly, he refused to have sex with her. She ended up feeling totally rejected and ugly. After the baby was born, he was captivated by his new daughter, proud of his wife, and wanted to love her again. To his dismay and confusion, she was not able to respond to his loving advances. In therapy, she was able to own how rejecting his comments had been.

When Two Become Three (or More)

Unplanned pregnancies often challenge the strength of a relationship, especially if one partner is delighted and the other ambivalent. A partner can feel very unforgiving when pressure to terminate a pregnancy is applied. In such circumstances, if the couple go ahead and have the baby, *how* they adapt to family life can often be affected negatively. Statistics (again, see Ganem, 2004) show that 75% of divorces occur within two years of the birth of a baby, and a common cause reported by the couples concerned was the lack of sexual contact during pregnancy. People are often surprised that a man can stray whilst his partner is pregnant. However, if a man has low self-esteem and feels pushed out, the temptation to cheat, if a situation presents itself, can sometimes prove to be hard to turn down. This may seem shocking, but it is by no means unusual.

Couples struggle with the experience of pregnancy and childbirth, and its effects upon family life, in different ways and with different levels of success. Most will get on with it and end up doing well enough. For some, however, problems become too great to bear and treatment is sought. The following case studies refer to clients who I have worked with. Names and details have been changed in order to protect client confidentiality.

Case 1

Scenario

Neil (31 years); Sarah (29 years); Married for 5 years: Young son aged 18 months

Fragmenting Family?

Background History:

Sarah: Her parents married young and have successfully brought up four children. All four have done well. Sarah described her childhood as "very happy", with Mum always being there for them. Dad worked hard, but still had time for his children and was very hands-on at weekends and holidays. Her parents are still active and currently help out with child-care and babysitting. At the time of coming to therapy, Sarah had returned to full-time work for financial reasons and Grandma was looking after 18 month old Tom during the working day.

Neil: His parents divorced when he was two years old and he was brought up by his mother and his stepfather. Contact with own father was spasmodic, owing to his father's job. Mum went on to have two other children. Neil gets on very well with his stepbrother and stepsister, but is not in regular contact with them, or his parents.

The Problem as Presented: No sex since Tom was born. Sarah had "gone off it." Neil described the marriage as being more like a "brother/sister" relationship: good friends who get on very well. They had tried to talk about it, but seemed to get nowhere. They both reported a good sexual relationship before Tom was born.

Neil and Sarah came to counselling as a result of a big row. They had previously rarely fallen out and it had given them both a wake-up call. Both were very upset and Neil was feeling aggrieved over his wife's reluctance to have sex or to try to get to the bottom of why it was not happening. Sarah described all the usual problems concerning working full-time and trying to be a good employee, wife and mother. She was tired most of the time and felt that Neil was being unreasonable. Sarah came from a very happy family, getting on really well with her two sisters and her brother. Her mum had loved being at home with the children and had provided a good role model for good parenting.

In contrast, Neil's parents had split up when he was young and his mum had remarried. He had little contact with his biological father and felt pushed out when two subsequent children (stepbrother and stepsister) were born to the new marriage. Neil's relationship with his wife had been "fantastic" (in his own words) and he would not have minded if they had not had children. Despite this, he agreed to the pregnancy and loved his son to bits and would not want to be without him. He also loved his wife's independence and her success at work. They had a good lifestyle, with plenty of holidays and a lovely home. With Grandma looking after their son during the working week, life was perfect.

However, during therapy it was soon clear that sex was not the main issue, but a symptom of his wife's distress at being a working mother. Sarah had not been able to share her growing resentment that her mother was bringing up her child. She felt ungrateful and selfish. She could not tell her mother how she felt, as it was not her mother's fault and she did not want to upset the family. Her anger was directed at Neil, as he was the cause of her needing to remain at work. She had never been able to share this with him, but had become increasingly withdrawn, until she no longer wanted to make love to him. Neil had no reason to believe that being a "stay-at-home" mum was part of her life-plan. He had been independent from his family from a very early age and did not see that it would hurt Tom, or Sarah, if she was not a full time mum.

Sarah explained that she had never felt that she had a choice in the matter. She was very successful in her job, and her husband, family and friends had all assumed that she would go back after the baby was born, with her mum set up to child-mind. At the time, it had not occurred to her that she would feel so different after Tom was born. Her husband was astonished to hear this, as he had assumed she was happy with the way things were and would want their comfortable life to continue the way it was.

The outcome of all of this was a renegotiation of finances, lifestyle and childcare. A solution was found which suited them all. Sarah negotiated with her employers to work part-time, and partly from home. She also found out that Grandma was actually finding looking after 18-month old Tom all week a bit too much. She also had not felt able to share this with her daughter. She was more than happy to do less child-minding.

Not only did communication improve between the couple, but the whole family benefited. Sarah's mum and dad also needed time for themselves, but they had felt unable to ask if they could take a step back from all the care and babysitting that they were doing. The wider family adjusted their lives to accommodate the changes. Sarah and Neil also had to deal with a drop in income, which meant fewer holidays and treats. By the end of therapy their communication had improved to such a degree that sex spontaneously returned after a night out celebrating their fifth wedding anniversary. Another bonus was the associated effects upon the wider family. It transpired that all of the family had taken Mum and Dad for granted. My client's two sisters and brothers also cut down their demands on their parents. By way of a thank you to their parents, they all contributed towards a well-earned holiday abroad for them in the sun. Overall, this was a very happy outcome for everyone concerned.

When Two Become Three (or More)

This case clearly illustrates how the experience of having a child can throw up feelings and emotions that might not have been expected before the event. Sarah did not realise how strong her maternal feelings would be before she gave birth to Tom. Good communication of expectations, hopes, and fears prior to giving birth (or perhaps even getting pregnant) can lessen the chances of such a situation arising and adversely affecting the relationship.

Case 2

Scenario

Max (39 years); Amanda (40 years); Married for 8 years: Young son aged 2 years

Background history:

Amanda: She was brought up in a very close, loving family. Her parents' relationship was described as "perfect". Amanda is very close to her father and was often called "Daddy's girl". She has one older sister, very practical, who runs her household and family with a minimum of fuss. Her sister was very close to her mother, as they are very alike.

Max: He was brought up in a traditional family. Max was one of three boys in a man's household. His mum was not physically affectionate, but the children knew that she loved them. Dad was quite strict, but there was a lot of good-natured play fighting and a shared love of sports. Sacrifices were made to send the boys to private school, and all three boys have done well in their chosen careers.

Fragmenting Family?

The Problem as Presented: Referred by a consultant at the local hospital, Amanda was reported as being depressed and anxious. She had "gone off" sex and was unsure about her relationship. The couple were still having sex at the time of referral, but she was not enjoying it. Their child was born through IVF treatment, but they were hoping to have a second child by natural means. Max had always wanted a large family.

Amanda and Max were much more complex than a first glance would suggest. Depression and anxiety after a much-wanted first child is not unusual. Also, IVF is a very stressful way to conceive a child and the couple really hoped that a second child could be conceived naturally. As a consequence, sex was still happening, but as a means to having another child, not for enjoyment, pleasure or any of the fun elements usually connected to adult sexual play.

It had been agreed that Amanda was well enough to come into therapy, despite her depression. Her consultant was of the view that, if they could sort out their problems then the depression would lift. She was not an easy client, being quite withdrawn at first. Max was far more motivated towards finding out the cause of her unhappiness and was willing to do whatever was required. I remember feeling quite surprised at her expression when he said this, but did not comment on this at the time.

On discussing their histories, it transpired that Amanda had always felt protected by her father, who would help her get out of household chores to spend time with him in the garden. Her mother and sister would always speak disparagingly of her domestic abilities, but she did not care. She enjoyed the time spent with her dad. As she grew up, she found herself comparing all of her boyfriends to her dad and finding them lacking. By her 30th birthday, she had almost given up hope of ever finding a partner.

Max, on the other hand, came from what he described as a traditional family. Everyone knew their place and their roles in the family. They were a happy, boisterous family, constantly outdoors. They kept numerous pets and had a mum who was not fussy about housework. Standards, however, were kept and manners were very important. Dad took care of Mum financially, and Mum took care of the domestic arrangements. He does not remember his dad doing much in the home.

When they met, Amanda felt that he was her knight in shining armour. Her parents took to Max immediately. He had a good job and came from a good family. They married on her 32nd birthday. They were both ready to settle down and start a family. When this did not happen their relationship floundered. Max was unable to talk about personal things (just like his dad) and Amanda was left bewildered when she did not get the emotional support she needed. Rather than fight this she turned to her dad. It was Dad who suggested they try IVF. When their son was born both families were thrilled. However, two years on she was not coping as a mum. All the jokes her mum and sister used to make about her seemed to Amanda to have come home to roost. She felt herself a failure, and even felt unable to talk to her dad about how bad she felt. Max was also disappointed. He thought he had married someone who could be as capable as her mum and sister. It had not mattered whilst they were on their own, but he now constantly felt exasperated by her lack of skills with the baby and her constant worrying. At the time of seeing her consultant, she was only speaking occasionally on the phone to her family and was very depressed. She was constantly anxious about the baby and whether or not he was thriving. Sex was the last thing on her mind; yet sex was happening. They had been told that often, after IVF treatment, the next child could come naturally.

I asked them what they wanted from therapy. Max said: "A happy sex life"; Amanda said that she did not know. What emerged, after many weeks of talking, was the lack of support that Amanda felt that she had received from her husband at the start of IVF treatment. It was as if it was all down to her and nothing to do with him. The loneliest times were when she needed to inject herself in the middle of the night. She felt totally rejected by him and later resentful that he was so proud of himself and his son, when he had played no part in the "difficult bits". As Paul Gilbert states:

> Lonely, despair-type depressions can arise when it seems that we cannot get close enough to others; we feel cut off and solitary. When people are depressed they often feel emotionally alone and isolated – this is part of the depressive experience. It can feel as if there is a barrier between oneself and others. (1997, p. 33)

Amanda's depression started at this point and, although she was able to mask it through the joy of pregnancy and Tom's birth, it never really left her. It was only finally diagnosed when she was referred to the consultant. Max found this very hard to take on board, but to his credit he did so. Amanda's story also explained her "look" at the start of therapy, when Max said that he would do anything to help sort things out.

Max and Amanda each took responsibility for their part in the breakdown. Max accepted that he had expected Amanda to be like her mum and sister, and recognised that his mother had been nothing like them, even though his own childhood had been very happy. He also admitted resenting her dad and his influence upon her. Max had been pleased when she saw less of him. He also agreed that, if they needed IVF again, it would be very different.

Amanda was able to admit that turning to her father had not helped, but had merely prevented her from being able to admit to herself that Max was not perfect and also to her disappointment with that fact.

This couple made huge changes. They made the decision to move to the other side of the country to be closer to Max's family. In their company, Amanda felt much less of a failure. She knew she would miss her dad, but the positives far outweighed the negatives. Max's mum's relaxed lifestyle suited her better. His brothers and their families accepted her with open arms and her son now had cousins to play with. She no longer felt depressed and incapable. Her husband was taking much more responsibility around the house and subsequently sex became enjoyable again. I had a card from them some time after therapy to announce the birth of their baby girl, conceived by natural means.

Case 3

Scenario

A second marriage for both parties; Lucy (two children from her first marriage: a girl aged 5 and a boy aged 8); Richard (three children from his first marriage: a boy aged 15 and two girls, aged 9 and 11); No children from this marriage[1]

---

[1] There is much information available for stepfamilies these days. I was fortunate enough to be able to draw on a lot of resources from the National Stepfamily Association when working with this couple.

Fragmenting Family?

Background history:

Lucy: She had experienced a very happy first marriage, until her husband developed cancer. Her daughter was only a few months old when he was diagnosed. He died before Lily reached the age of two. Her son, Daniel, was very badly affected by his father's death and developed behavioural problems. These lasted for many months. Daniel also reacted badly to Richard, but soon settled down once Richard had moved in. Lucy was pleased when Daniel agreed to be a pageboy at their wedding six months ago.

Richard: His first wife had had an affair with his best friend whilst he was away in the Army. She had originally travelled abroad with him, but wanted the children to have a more settled schooling and disapproved of boarding schools, so he went abroad without her. He found out about the affair when his youngest daughter talked about how his friend stayed the night. His wife admitted that the affair had been going on for a long time and that she wanted a divorce. Richard immediately got a posting abroad and saw his children infrequently. He met his new wife Lucy at a New Year's Eve party and eventually decided he was ready to settle down again. He came out of the Army and the couple now live together with her children.

The Problem as Presented: Lucy would like to have a child with Richard, but he feels they have enough problems with the children they already have.

For Richard and Lucy the baby was an issue before it was even conceived. Lucy saw it as an extension of her love for

Richard. He did not feel able to cope with another child, especially as he had to build enormous bridges with his own three children. This was because of his long absences abroad during his Army career. At the time of entering into therapy, their domestic arrangements were based on his children coming every other weekend from Friday until Sunday afternoon. Lucy's children wanted to get on with their stepsiblings and were often upset by an apparent lack of interest in them. Lucy's son especially admired his 15-year-old stepbrother and was desperate for any signs of interest from him. Her daughter, aged 5, wanted to be included by her two stepsisters in their games, but they often sent her away. Lucy explained to her children how hard it was for the other children to be away from their own mum, and had asked for patience.

When I asked them what they hoped for from therapy, she responded quickly by saying that she hoped I would help him to see that a new baby could unite them all as a family. His response was very different. Whilst Richard recognised her contribution to making the weekends when his children came to stay a success, he was finding it hard to connect with them himself. He had been away for such a huge part of their growing up (this was especially true of his son) that he felt another baby would alienate them further, rather than bring them together. His middle child had already commented that he "spoilt" the 5-year-old by giving in to her when she asked to play with them and he insisted that they let her join in.

At this point, it became clear that a new baby was the least of their worries and that establishing how this current family could function seemed to be more of a priority. They both agreed to look at this issue first.

What transpired over the following months was that this couple renegotiated their expectations and hopes for themselves and their family. Lucy needed to look at the legacy of her first marriage. She had lost a dear husband and had struggled to be there for her children during a most distressing time for all of the family. In order to cope with the loss she became very busy and practical, never taking the time to grieve. Now she was expecting her new husband to help take away the painful memories of those first weeks and months after her daughter was born. With her first husband so ill, she had not been able to enjoy her new daughter. Now she wanted a new baby with Richard to take away that pain and to create a new experience as far removed as possible from the one she had had when her previous husband was dying. This was a role Richard was not ready for. She also admitted that Richard's children were a strain, and that it was hard for her to stay positive when they came to stay. They did not always like her cooking and constantly argued over what time they should go to bed. Mostly, she coped well with the situation, but as Richard was terrified of upsetting his children, he was of no real help. As a consequence, she often had to prepare food to keep them happy and accept that they would stay up late.

For Richard, it was as much about trust as anything else. He had also not really got over the shock of loss and betrayal by his first wife. In fact, it was this that was making it even harder for him to relate to his children. His daughters looked like their mother, and even his son had her mannerisms. Although he loved them, he was finding it easier to relate to Lucy's children than his own. They did not remind him of the past. With her son, he felt he had a second chance, and her daughter had been so young when he appeared on the scene that she treated him like her real dad. Exploring all this through the counselling helped them to recognise just how much baggage they had each brought into the relationship. Together, they agreed that they needed to help their five children mix together more and that once a fortnight was not enough. Although this meant contact with Richard's ex-wife, whom he detested, it was agreed that this was necessary in order to integrate his children into the family in a more inclusive, more positive way. "Ideally, everyone needs to be involved in the decision-making process in order for discipline to be effective. Adults must take responsibility for making the final decisions, but children must be heard too." (Kahn, 1995, p. 112). They agreed to hold a family "round table", for all to have a say in how the family should run.

They subsequently reported back to me that it had gone extremely well. Richard's three children had welcomed the opportunity to say what they would like from their visits and from their father. They had felt his distance and were happy to have him be more involved. He agreed to see his children for after-school activities, and even agreed to participate in activities that Lucy's children could enjoy as well. Swimming seemed to be their main activity of interest, except for the eldest, so a weekly trip to the local swimming pool was a start. A huge step forward was the prospect of a new house, which would provide the 15-year -old with his own room. With increased contact and access during the week, the family started to feel more like a real family. They also drew up a new set of rules about bedtimes and mealtimes. This had helped to take the stress out of their visits. The children helped plan menus that they could all try and enjoy, and also did some of the cooking! Lucy said the mess at first had been hard to deal with, but the pay-off was that all of the children ate the same food. At the end of therapy, the baby was on hold whilst this new family got to grips with the new arrangements. They still had a long way to go, but at least they were now on the right path.

Case 4

Scenario

A lesbian couple; Shelley (31 years); Ann (33 years; three children from a brief marriage when aged 20: twins aged 13 and a daughter aged 11); Partners for 6 years

Background history:

Ann: Previously married to an older man when she was 20, Ann had quickly realised that this was a big mistake but, after an unplanned pregnancy, gave birth to the twins soon afterwards and decided to make the best of things for the sake of the children. Her third daughter was also unplanned. Her husband worked away a lot and this helped her cope with her undisclosed sexual orientation. Then she met Shelley at a local drama group and fell hopelessly in love. She had never felt like this with her husband. She told Shelley how she felt and that she was willing to leave her husband for her.

Shelley: Openly gay, her sexual orientation was accepted by her family. She had had several longish-term relationships, but had never lived fully with another woman. She had been concerned that Ann had never been "out" on the gay scene, and questioned her sexuality. She was also fearful of Ann leaving her family to move in with her. Would she change her mind? Did Shelley need this? In the event, Ann left her family and bought a small property near her ex-husband so that she could see the children every day. Shelley eventually moved in with Ann, keeping her own place as a safety net.

When Two Become Three (or More)

The Problem as Presented: Two issues were presented:

1) Shelley's desire to have a child of her own, and;
2) Shelley's university course.

When I first met Ann and Shelley they were at crisis point. Ann was jealous of the time Shelley was spending with other students on her course and feeling left out. Shelley countered that Ann spent a lot of time dealing with problems that her children had and entertaining them. She did not see why she should always have to sit around waiting for Ann to come back from her ex-husband's house, which could be as late as 8 or 9 o'clock in the evening. As Ann often cooked for the children, Shelley was left to eat alone. Their sex life was suffering and this made both women feel vulnerable and afraid that the relationship would end. Shelley found it hard to understand Ann's jealousy. However, Nancy Friday offers the Oxford University definition of this emotion: "Jealous: ... in love or affection, especially in sexual love". Her definition continues: "Apprehensive of being displaced in the love or good-will of someone; distrustful of the faithfulness of wife, husband, or lover." (Friday, 1986, p. 26). Ann had not been involved in the gay scene, but she had her own ideas of how it worked. Her fear was that Shelley would have casual sex with one of her gay student friends. Could she really trust her?

Furthermore, there were other factors impacting on them as a couple. Ann's parents had rejected her since she had left her husband. They were appalled by the fact that she was living with another woman and had refused to meet Shelley. As a consequence Ann had broken off all contact with her parents. They now gave all their support to her husband and helped him to take care of the children.

Her husband had also reacted badly at first, refusing access to the children and changing his job so that he could be at home more for them. He also did not want the children to go to Ann's new home. Ann was working on this, but the strain was beginning to show. She had naively assumed everyone would accept her choice and be happy for her. The break-up of her marriage had been awful for her whole family, including the children. She felt she had given up so much for Shelley and needed Shelley to support her fight for the children. Initially, Shelley was happy to do this, but the lonelier she felt, the more she turned to her university friends for companionship.

The other issue was Shelley's age. She felt that time was moving on and she had always wanted a child of her own. She had always thought she would go for AID [Artificial Insemination by Donor] before she was 30 but, because of Ann's fight for her own children, she had put it on hold. She now felt that, with their relationship so unstable, her only choice would be to return to her own house and have a baby on her own. Her family had always said they would help her through a pregnancy and birth.

Ann was torn, desperately wanting her own children to live with them for some of the time. How could she think of another child? This couple were being broken apart by the situation they found themselves in. They had forgotten what they had meant to each other and how they needed to talk openly of their hopes, fears, expectations, and the future. During therapy, they began to open up to each other and, instead of being overwhelmed by the whole messy situation, they started to break problems down into smaller, more manageable sections.

Ann's ex-husband had found a new partner who also had children. She was much more understanding of Ann's situation and encouraged Ann's ex-husband to let the children visit Ann at her home. The girls got on really well

198

with Shelley. They liked her style. Soon they were staying over, which in turn gave Ann's ex-husband a break to spend time with his new partner. As things at home started to settle, Shelley found that she did not need to stay out with her university friends so often. Ann's intensely jealous feelings began to subside as she began to trust Shelley. They began to have family meals together and, when the topic of a new baby for Shelley came up, the twins said, "Go for it!" Ann and Shelley were closer than ever and sex was as good as it had been at the beginning of their relationship.

This case clearly illustrates the changes in the nature of family life and society as a whole. It is much more acceptable for gay parents to have children of their own and for their children to grow up without the stigma that was previously attached to such unions. Sadly for Ann, by the end of the treatment her parents were still not willing to meet up with Shelley, although they were now speaking to Ann on the phone.

Changes in society can often be especially unpalatable for the older generation and it may be that Ann's parents will never accept their daughter's sexuality or her relationship. However, Ann and Shelley both hope that, with time, they will see that they were missing out on what was now a close family unit, especially with the prospect of a new baby in the future. For this couple, the problems stretch much wider than just coping with a new baby, and conceiving through a donor will really test their love and commitment to each other.

Case 5

Scenario

A married couple, together for 20 years and married for 15 years; Tracey (35 years); Phil (36 years); Young daughter aged 16 months

Background History:

Tracey: Tracey was from a working-class background with no expectations. She began work as an office junior straight from school. She married at 20 after a four year engagement. She discovered that she was good with figures and soon found herself promoted at work. She gained confidence and started studying accountancy at evening classes with the help of her company and the support of Phil. She moved jobs to gain further promotions and eventually she was head-hunted by a large accountancy firm in the City.

Phil: Phil had lived in the same street as Tracey and went to the same school. Their families were close friends. He had always liked Tracey and was delighted when she agreed to go out with him. He did not do so well at school academically and left early to join his dad on a building site. He learned all aspects of construction and became a very good bricklayer. His expectations were that they would settle down near their families and have children of their own. He was thrilled when little Rosie was born and devoted all of his spare time to looking after her. As his wife was often late home, they employed a nanny who came in daily. She left as soon as Phil came home.

When Two Become Three (or More)

The Problem as Presented: A friend had recommended counselling as this couple were drifting apart and were often arguing when together. Tracey had taken minimal time off work when Rosie was born and was back working full time. The nanny did not live in. This was not something Phil could deal with (none of his or her family had ever had paid help). This was often at the root of their many rows. She earned more in bonuses than he earned in a year and was suggesting that, if he did not like having the nanny in the house, then he should stay at home to look after Rosie.

This case was interesting as it challenged established gender roles and responsibilities. This couple came from ordinary working-class backgrounds in which Dad went out to work and Mum stayed at home. However, during counselling it was discovered that both mums eventually worked as well to help make ends meet. Neither set of parents had high expectations for their children academically and just wanted them to be happy. Tracey's parents were astonished at her success at work. Her desire to succeed and go back to work after Rosie was born was as mystifying to Phil's parents as it was to her own. Both sets of parents had been so happy that this young couple had got together because of their long established family friendship.

As Tracey's pay packet increased, their lifestyle changed. They were able to buy a home of their own, something neither of their parents had done. They could afford nice holidays and all the trappings that money could buy to make life comfortable. After one large bonus they took both families, including Tracey's older brother and sisters, abroad to celebrate her parents' ruby wedding anniversary.

Having Rosie was a big deal for both partners. It gave Phil the child he had longed for, but it was a huge sacrifice for Tracey, given her chosen career path. She knew that she would have to get back to work as quickly as possible if she was not to lose any of the advantages she had built up. She loved Rosie, but did not feel particularly maternal with regard to staying at home with her, rather than working. She liked making what she called "quality time" for her daughter and was glad to be able to provide her with nice clothes and toys. Tracey was happy with the current set-up, but she also knew that Phil did not want "a stranger" bringing up their child. Their rows were usually over this topic, especially if the nanny had done something he did not like.

It was amazing that this couple were together at all. She presented herself as the successful businesswoman she undoubtedly was, smart and well dressed, whereas he often came to sessions in his working clothes, apologising for his "mucky boots". However, as time progressed it was clear that they still had a lot of love for each other and were able to appreciate the other's differences. Tracey felt that he helped her to keep her feet on the ground, as she met a lot of ruthless and insincere people in her job. She had seen lots of relationships breakdown through affairs at work, and also through people working too hard. She felt that Phil was steadfast and reliable, solid and dependable. She loved that about him. She trusted him and knew he would never hurt her.

Phil, on the other hand, admired her abilities and never seemed to resent them. He had encouraged her first attempts at evening classes and even cooked meals for her after a hard day's work on a building site so that she could study. They regarded themselves as a team. Things only deteriorated when he asked her when they were going to start a family. Tracey had put it off and continued to put it off. She just had to do this project or go for that promotion; they were young, they had time. He had accepted this but, when their siblings started producing babies, he had become broody. Phil wanted to have a child of his own. He loved his nieces and nephews and enjoyed it when he and Tracey were able to take them for treats and nice days out. He also loved Christmas. They still went to his parents on Christmas Day and loved seeing the children's faces when they opened their presents. Tracey eventually relented and was fortunate enough to become pregnant straight away.

Tracey worked for as long as possible during her pregnancy and went back to work after only four weeks. She asked for work to be sent home to her throughout this time. Rosie was a good baby and a nanny was employed before she went back to work to make certain she was the right person for the job. Phil, despite liking the nanny, did not really want her in the house. However, he could not persuade Tracey to give up work, or even to go part-time. As the rows got worse a friend suggested counselling. It was during counselling that Tracey presented the idea of Phil being a house husband. This was an alien concept to him, as he believed that "real men" worked. Both his brothers worked, while their wives stayed at home whilst the babies were small, taking on part-time work only when the children went to school. The idea that he should stay at home to look after Rosie seemed "daft" to him.

However, they started talking it through and, instead of turning it into an argument, they looked at the pros and cons of such a change. The fact that it did not need to be forever, the fact that work was always a problem through the winter months for him, the fact that he loved spending time with Rosie taking her swimming and to the park, all favoured the proposed change. The housework was a bit of an issue, but even that could be dealt with if they employed someone to clean once or twice a week. Financially, it was not a problem. They could easily live on her income. Support came from a surprising quarter. One of Phil's brothers said, given the option, he would love to be able to give up his boring, repetitive job to stay at home with his kids. Unfortunately, both he and his wife had to work to keep up with their mortgage payments. He did not see much of his wife as, when he got in, she went out to an evening job. The client started to realise that this was an opportunity.

They finally agreed to give it a trial period. Phil knew that he was a good "brickie" and had a good reputation with local companies. He could always return to work if the trial did not work out. We agreed a follow-up session in three months to see how they had fared.

When I next met up with Tracey and Phil, they were two months into the change and Phil had taken to it like a duck to water. Both of their mums were happy for him to drive over and visit, as were all the siblings. He attended a Mothers and Toddlers Group once a week, as suggested by the health visitor, and was quite a hit amongst the mums. All his notions of what makes a man had been turned upside down. He had surprised himself at how efficient he was around the house and how Rosie responded well to her new routine. Tracey was also thrilled. She came home to an un-grumpy husband and they enjoyed dinner together, relaxing and talking over a glass of wine. They had a family holiday planned for the three of them in the summer.

Tracey was full of praise for how he had coped when Rosie had come down with a sickness bug. Their communication was better than it had ever been. Phil was able to tell her to "back off" when she sometimes tried to take over, and Tracey was able to tell him when she needed time with her daughter for herself. This couple had come a long way from their roots. Neither of their fathers would have taken this role on and it was a cause of much hilarity when discussed within the family. As things were going so well for her at work (she felt her position in the company was assured), they were discussing giving Rosie a little brother or sister within the next year or so. Phil was delighted, as one child did not match up to his idea of what a family was. With their new communication skills to help, I was certain that this couple would do well. Living a different life from what you have been brought up to expect is a huge challenge. This couple had more than proved that it is possible.

Discussion

These cases clearly illustrate that becoming new parents or creating a family around existing children can be highly stressful. Family values, norms and belief systems, untested by a new couple in love, gradually start to impact on the challenges we all face on a daily basis. Who does what, when? Couples who bring past relationship "baggage" with them into a new relationship face even bigger challenges. As we have seen, seemingly simple matters such as food and bedtime (Case 3) can become a battlefield. Adjusting to different expectations can be difficult if the couple do not communicate clearly. Patriarchy can rear its head and a woman suddenly finds that she is financially dependent on her husband. Alternatively, a man may be challenged to be a house husband because his wife has the greater earning potential (Case 5).

Remarriage can often be difficult where one partner has divorced and the other is bereaved (Case 3). Roles can be assigned that are not wanted. Loss and change are part of life, because without them, how would we know when we are happy. Adapting to change, however, can be affected by whether the change is wanted and planned for, or unexpected and not wanted. Leaving her baby at home with her mother was not what my client (Case 1) wanted, and yet she could not find the words to share her concerns with her husband. Communication is the key to finding solutions to problems but, as we all know, it is not always easy to find the right time, the right words, or even to understand yourself with regard to what needs to be communicated. You simply know things are not right.

We are heavily influenced by our own family backgrounds: how our parents treated us, how close or distant they were, how loving or otherwise, how caring or affectionate. Having a very close bond with a parent (Case 2) can set up impossibly high standards for a new partner. Equally, having a poor relationship with parents can sometimes make it hard to bond with others and even our own children. Attachment theory tells us that we all need a "secure base" (Bowlby, 1979 p. 136) in order to be able to trust and to put our trust in others. Nowhere is that more apparent than when a couple decide to have a baby together. All our hopes, expectations and longings come to the fore when we reproduce. Having good support can turn a negative situation into a positive experience. I was very heartened by a recent article about the "Single Mum of the Year Award". Despite an early teenage pregnancy, the award had been made to a young woman who had brought up her child alone, gone back to school and completed a university education. At the time of the award she was in a stable relationship with a second child and a good job. This strongly suggests that difficult beginnings do not always lead to disaster. Having someone believe in you and encourage you to reach your full potential can bring forward real rewards and happiness.

We live in an age of enormous change, with new technology hitting us from all sides. The speed with which news is relayed around the world has changed our perceptions. We see on television the realities of fragmented families on a daily basis: abuse, violence, family breakdown, separation and divorce. "Soaps" claim to reflect "real life", but the speed with which their characters recover from tragedy on the screen desensitises us to the pain and violence we see enacted. Also, we can switch the television off. It is only when tragedy strikes on a personal level that it makes a full impact. Sadly, there are many suffering families out there that need help. I hope that my contribution has brought with it some optimism and the hope that people can adjust and rise to the challenges of new situations, not least when two become three.

References

Bowlby, J. (1979). *The making and breaking of affectional bonds.* London: Tavistock/Routledge.

Ford, V. (2005). *Overcoming sexual problems: A self-help guide using cognitive behavioral techniques.* London: Robinson.

Friday, N. (1986). *Jealousy.* London: Collins.

Ganem, M. (2004, May). *Pregnancy and sexuality.* Paper presented at the European Sexology Conference, Brighton.
Abstract: In *Sexual and Relationship Therapy, 19* (2, Supp. 1), S14.

Gilbert, P. (1997). *Overcoming depression: A self-help guide using cognitive behavioral techniques.* London: Robinson.

Kahn, T. (1995) *Learning to step together: Building and strengthening stepfamilies: A handbook for step-parents and parents.* London: National Stepfamily Association.

Martyn, E. (2001). *Baby shock!: Your relationship survival guide.* London: Vermilion, in conjunction with Relate.

Office for National Statistics. (2005). *2001 census: General report for England and Wales.* Basingstoke: Palgrave Macmillan.

Winnicott, D. W. (1971) Transitional objects and transitional phenomena. In D. W. Winnicott, *Playing and reality* (pp. 1-25). London: Tavistock/Routledge.

Additional Reading

Bowlby, J. (1976). *Child care and the growth of love* (M. Fry, Ed.). (2nd ed.). London: Penguin.

Dalton, K. (1989). *Depression after childbirth: How to recognize and treat postnatal illness.* (2nd ed.). Oxford: Oxford University Press.

Gerhardt, S. (2004). *Why love matters: How affection shapes a baby's brain.* Hove: Brunner-Routledge.

Murray Parkes, C., Stevenson-Hinde, J., & Marris, P. (Eds.). (1991). *Attachment across the life cycle.* London: Tavistock/Routledge.

Salisbury, C., & Walters, C. (1997). *All together now: What to expect when stepfamilies get together.* London: Stepfamily Publications.